POEMS AND SONGS

BY

ROBERT CROSBIE.

———————

"E'en then a wish, I mind its pow'r,
A wish that to my latest hour
    Shall strongly heave my breast, —
That I, for poor auld Scotland's sake,
Some usefu' plan or book could make,
    Or sing a sang at least."
               BURNS.

———————

PRINTED AND PUBLISHED FOR THE AUTHOR BY
W. SMITH ELLIOT,
HIGH STREET, GALASHIELS.
1888.

PREFACE.

———•◦❀◦•———

In issuing from the Press this Second Edition of Poems, Songs, &c., it may be stated that a long interval has elapsed since the first small volume appeared, copies of which have been in request for some time back ; and when none were to be had, the author, at the request of numerous friends, has now ventured to publish the present volume, revised and enlarged, and would humbly indulge the hope that it may be received with some degree of favour and acceptance in its new dress.

We now take the opportunity of returning sincere and grateful thanks to our numerous subscribers, and to each and all who have kindly interested themselves in its success.

ROBERT CROSBIE.

Innerleithen.

CONTENTS.

———••◦◦◦••———

Poems and Songs.

THE COTTAGE FLOWERS.

"And slight withal may be the things which bring
Back on the heart the weight which it would fling
Aside for ever."

PART FIRST.

REMOTE within a peaceful glen,
Far from the busy haunts of men,
  In bygone years there stood
A cot, whose ruins still are seen,
As relics yet of what have been
  In that wild solitude.

Sweet honeysuckle round the door
Still clings, as in the days of yore,
  Where hangs a simple tale;
Which they who read will joy that e'er
The beauteous flowers grew up there,
  In sweetness to the gale.

A happy couple lived serene
For many a year amid the scene,
       Nor dream'd of aught below
That could intrude, and there annoy
Or mar their peace and lasting joy,
       And fill their hearts with woe.

An only daughter was their pride ;
And there, at summer's evening tide,
       Before the cottage-door,
Sweet Lucy dress'd their plants and flowers,
While they would sit, and view for hours
       Their beauties o'er and o'er.

Thus pass'd their tranquil evening hours,
And for sweet Lucy, 'mong the flowers,
     They would in secret pray,
That He who decks the lilies fair
Would make her His peculiar care,
       And guide her steps alway

Retired within their humble cot,
The world and all its cares forgot,
       How sweet was their repose !
And when the morning sun had drest
The eastern sky in crimson vest,
       How cheerful they arose !

Forth to the labours of the day,
The sire each morning took his way,
　　With health and spirits light;
Far from the city's sad turmoils,
Contentment crown'd his daily toils,
　　And slumbers sweet by night

Thus years passed on, and Lucy grew
To womanhood, and there were few
　　That could with her compare.
No artist's pencil e'er could trace
The features of a lovely face
　　So sweet, so passing fair.

Rear'd in a glen, yet there refined
She grew, with cultivated mind,
　　And every witching grace;
But of the world she little knew,
Itsbright side only she could view,
　　Through nature's smiling face.

Ah! enviable days, I ween,
Were hers, amid the rural scene,
　　That like an Eden smiled;
But there the tempter came at last,
And clouds of grief were gath'ring fast,
　　For Lucy was beguiled.

And often in the twilight grey
Was Lucy sèen, upon her way
　　To meet a coming form ;
A wretch, a villain in disguise,
Deceitful as the laughing skies
　　Before a coming storm.

Well skill'd was he in every art
To win her warm confiding heart,
　　And to her listening ear
His words came, as a charm that bound
Her heart to him in love profound,
　　And banish'd every fear.

Ye virtuous ones, that eye with scorn
A sister ruined and forlorn,
　　Take heed, your censure spare,
Lest you, in an unguarded hour,
May fall, like her, beneath the power
　　Of some false lover's snare.

With beating heart and watchful eye,
An anxious mother soon did spy
　　Her daughter's alter'd mien ;
And to her painful questions plied,
Poor Lucy sat, and but replied
　　With sighs, and sobs between.

But, as a willing captive chain'd,
True to her love she still remain'd;
    And falsehood first knew she,
When her false lover fail'd to meet
Her often in the loved retreat,
    Beside the trysting-tree.

And long she often waited there,
With heart nigh broken in despair,
    While mocking night winds sigh'd;
As Lucy there, in shame and grief,
Thought she could only find relief,
    If there she could have died.

And when her sighs and tears were spent,
Slow, down the glen poor Lucy went,
    Sad, silent, and alone,
Till, half unconscious, she drew near
The cot, that now no more could cheer;
    Joys there seem'd ever gone.

'Tis true, two doating hearts were there,
Who loved her, with that pious care
    Which parents only know;
But one idea fix'd her soul,
And oft whole nights without control
    The bitter tears did flow.

Yet oft she wander'd to the spot—
That spot by lovers ne'er forgot—
    Where first their vows was given ;
And there once more they met to stray—
By what decree, let others say—
    Fate's, or the will of Heaven.

But how describe her sad divorce
From virtue, and her downward course,
    Led by the worst of men !
Away that night with him she fled,
To where he promised soon to wed
    Fair Lucy of the glen.

And who can paint the anguish felt
By two fond parents, as they knelt
    Within that humble cot!
In vain they look'd for her return,
And many a night and cheerless morn
    They sought, but found her not.

PART SECOND.

Long years had slowly pass'd away,
And two bent forms, with locks grown grey
    Still lived within that cot.

Their long-lost daughter yet they mourn'd,
For Lucy never had returned
To that now lonely spot.

That she was dead they now believed,
And even the thought their hearts relieved:
    'Twas better far, I ween,
Thus they thought, than had they known
The depth poor Lucy had been thrown
      And what for years had been.

Far in the city's crowded street,
To view her ruin now complete,
    To her we turn again;
Deserted there, and left betray'd,
Ah! how unlike the virtuous maid
      That lived within the glen.

Among the lowest of her sex,
There see her now familiar mix
    In paths of sin and shame;
The blush had left her beauteous cheek,
That once told more than words can speak
      Love's pure and virtuous flame.

And there she wander'd many a day,
To want and wretchedness a prey,
    With no kind friend to cheer;

When all her arts to lure had fail'd,
Her heart within her often quail'd,
    And forced the bitter tear.

'Twas on a smiling summer's morn,
That thus she wander'd out forlorn,
    And met upon her way,
In home-spun garb, a country boy,
His face lit up with health and joy,
    To see the city gay.

With buoyant step he march'd along,
Blithe as the lark, whose early song
    Had cheer'd his morning hours;
Sweet fragrance round him filled the air,
For in his hand he held with care
A beatuous bunch of flowers.

Sweet honeysuckle were the flowers,
Cull'd fresh that morn 'neath dewy showers,
    So pure, so bright and fair;
And as the rustic youth drew near,
Low stifled sobs fell on his ear,
    And sounds of deep despair.

And there the rustic, with surprise,
Beheld poor Lucy, while her eyes
    Were swimming deep in tears;

The well-known flowers had caught her gaze,
Companions of her early days,
    In happy by-gone years.

" Oh ! give the flowers to me," she cried,
As from her cheek she vainly tried
    To wipe her tears away.
"Sweet flowers! that deck'd the cottage door
Which I can scarce hope to see more—
    Oh! give me them, I pray."

Her bosom with emotion heaved,
As she the beauteous gift received,
    And bless'd the country boy ;
And while she press'd them to her heart,
They seem'd as if to ease the smart,
    And yield her sudden joy.

With fixed eyes upraised to Heaven,
She pray'd that hour to be forgiven—
    Nor was the prayer in vain.
She left the city that same hour,
And kiss'd the potent little flower
    Again, and yet again.

With hurried step upon her way,
Poor Lucy journey'd all that day,
    And wearied at its close,

THE COTTAGE FLOWERS.

Was fain to lay her aching head
Within a way-side humble shed,
    And seek the night's repose

In broken sleep she pass'd the night,
But, when the morn rose calm and bright,
    O'er moor and mossy fen,
A humble penitent sincere,
She sought the home once held so dear—
    The cottage in the glen.

And sure bright spirits from above
Would bend with placid looks of love,
    As homeward now she trod;
And on that flower admiring gaze,
That turn'd her from her evil ways,
    To virtue and to God.

O'er many a long and weary mile,
Poor Lucy, wand'ring, reach'd the stile
    Where often she had met
With him, the cause of all her woe,
And tears again began to flow,
    With painful, sad regret.

With faltering step, she soon drew near
Her childhood's home, in hope and fear
    Where sat the aged pair,

As they were wont, in the old seat
Outside the door, in summer's heat,
    To breathe the cooling air.

To greet the stranger on her way,
They rose, but how can words portray
    The scene, the shriek so wild,
When recognised, as in alarms
They eager rush'd, with open arms,
    And clasp'd their long-lost child!

And round their cottage door still cling
The flowers, whose influence I sing,
    To gild this simple tale,
Which they who read will joy that e'er
The beauteous flowers grew up there,
    In sweetness to the gale.

THE STREAMLET.

WANDERING little streamlet!
  Onward to the sea,
In thy course sae merrily
  Sparkling ever free;
To thy witching wavelets
  Ilk flower by thy side
Stoops, as if a-wooing
  A wee fairy bride.

Wily little streamlet!
  Gliding on sae slee,
In thy beauty winding
  Round ilk bush and tree;
Hid beneath the branches,
  Sunbeams woo in vain,
Till thy beauteous waters
  Sparkle out again.

Singing little streamlet!
  Murmuring along,

Staying here and listening
　To thy rippling song,
We, as if enchanted,
　Dream, or think we hear
More than earthly music
　Falling on our ear.

Faithful little streamlet !
　Ever from thy source
To the ocean's bosom
　Keeping in thy course.
Passing scenes of beauty,
　Flowers of every hue,
On we see thee journey,
　Murmuring " adieu."

Passing little streamlet '
　Life is like thy tide,
Careless, and as swiftly,
　Onward do we glide ;
And, methinks, thy murmurs
　Whispering, seem to say—
" Life here is vanity,
　Thus you pass away."

Beauteous little streamlet !
　Rippling to the main,

What may be thy features
 'Ere we meet again!
As tears, shower'd in sadness
 From a sky in gloom,
O'er us as we slumber
 In an early tomb.

SONNET.—TO THE SKYLARK.

SWEET minstrel, soaring to the clear blue sky,
    What happy thoughts inspire thee thus to sing!
    Thou seem'st to spurn the earth on outstretch'd
        wing,
A bright spirit mounting to its home on high.
    Far from this jarring world of noise and strife,
Who is there would not wish with thee to fly,
And leave those pleasures which must fade and
        die,
    With mortals here who vainly call them life?
From yonder sky, so tranquil and serene,
    Thy music falls as sunshine o'er the heart;
What are our highest strains but worthless,
        mean,
    Compared with thine in simple native art.
Sing on, sweet bird: O that our hearts were
        given—
Guileless and free as thine from earth to heaven.

S P R I N G.

COME where the water pours
Music and sparkling showers,
Over the crags where the woodlands now ring ,
    With a burst of delight,
    That cold winter takes flight,
While in his stead smiles the sweet blushing
    Spring.

    To his home in the north,
    Winter's over the Forth,
And we bid thee adieu, thou surly old king ,
    For the flowers with thy breath
    Were left wither'd in death,
But now they shall live, the fair children of
    Spring.

    Soon when the morning dawns,
    Bright o'er the smiling lawns,
To each grassy blade a dew-drop shall cling;
    Flow'rets shall rise and wave,
    Each o'er its wintry grave,
In the soft breezes of life-giving Spring,

A bright spirit of love,
Seems as if from above
Descending to earth on hovering wing,
Bidding nature rejoice,
Though we hear not its voice,
O sweet is the language of beautiful Spring.

Up o'er the forest dells,
Hark how the chorus swells,
From the gay throng as they merrily sing;
While to the sunny sky,
Far springs the lark on high,
Warbling its welcome to heart-cheering Spring

We, too, would join the strain—
Welcome thee back again.
Sweet are the gifts you so lavishly fling;
Over the smiling land,
Touch'd as with magic wand,
Nature, exulting, proclaims it is Spring.

S O N G.

O THINK na I can ever gang
    Frae Scotland, and frae thee, Mary :
I've lo'ed ye baith owre weel and lang,
    To sail across the sea, Mary.

Though nature spread 'neath foreign skies
    Scenes that are fair to view, Mary,
There's nought can ever break the ties
    That bind me still wi' you, Mary.

Let others boast their golden fields,
    Sae dazzlin' to their een, Mary,
The social joys Auld Scotia yields
    Are better far, I ween, Mary.

The land that wails in slav'ry's chain
    Is no the land for me, Mary.
The soil they tread shall never stain
    The foot I claim as free, Mary.

The heather grows na on their hills.
    The lintie sings na there, Mary ;
Nae flower-bells wave beside the rills,
    As in our land sae fair, Mary.

I wadna leave Auld Scotia's shore,
   For a' that wealth could gie, Mary.
Between us ocean ne'er shall roar ;
   In her I'll live and dee, Mary.

SONNET.—TO ABBOTSFORD.

HAIL, Abbotsford! where Scotland's minstrel sung,
   Whose memory and name shall still be dear,
   And claim the sacred homage of a tear,
O'er a sweet harp that now lies mute, unstrung ;
   Whose magic strains made new creations rise,
Refined the vulgar taste to fancy bright,
As sunshine gleaming through the shades of night
   Clothes the dim forms in beauty's fairest dyes.
Here would I musing sit, or pensive stray
   Where Tweed's bright waters lave their rocky
      bed
In moaning waves, and murmur on their way,
   As if they mourn'd the mighty spirit fled ;
While sighing breezes sweeping down the vale,
Seem to respond the melancholy wail.

TO A BOY.

Rich blessings on thee, darling boy!
Thy father's pride, thy mother's joy
  Oh may'st thou ever be.
God grant thee health with length of days;
And be thy guide in all thy ways,
  And still keep watch o'er thee.
So little pilgrim wend thy way
Through life, nor fear the darkest day,
  Nor aught than can befall ,
Through confidence by God sustained,
Thou'lt reach the mark to be attained,
  And more than conquer all.

TIME.

Passing ever,
  Staying never,
Phantom of an endless river,
  In silent, steady motion,
On whose dark unfathomed tide,
The wreck of ages, onward glide,
  To a shoreless ocean.

WINTER.

Weary auld winter,
Dreary cauld winter;
Pensive I sit here, so pensive I'll sing;
For few are the pleasures
And few are the treasures
To the poor of the land thou do'st ever bring.

God pity the poor,
Each day at our door;
To feed them, and cleed them, I want not the will.
But how to relieve them
Wi' naething to give them;
O', stir up the wealthy the task to fulfil.

Weary auld winter,
Deary cauld winter;
Cauld blaws the blast over muirland and lea,
But caulder the heart is,
And ill-dune their pairt is,
Wha hae plenty to spare, and naething to gie.

Ae thing wi' anither,
And ta'en a' thegether,
A strange world we live in o' sorrow and sin,
Some revellin' in riches—
Some starved as puir wretches;
To aim at description, 'twere vain to begin.

Weary auld winter,
Dreary cauld winter;
The time will sune come when 'tis a' the same
thing
That we live here in splendour,
Or, as beggars, we wander;
The dust you now tread on perhaps was a king.

Then patience attend us,
And heaven still send us
Oor comforts nae waur than what they ha'e
been;
And we'll warstle through life,
Though our hardships be rife;
May the days yet to come be the best we ha'e
seen.

Weary auld winter,
Dreary cauld winter;
There are pleasures in store yet, and to them I'll
cling,
When thy dark days are over,
Thro' green fields a rover,
I'll hail the sweet pleasures and blessings of
Spring.

A GALASHIELS WORTHIE.

An honest auld worthie was queer Willie a' Thing.
If ever ye wanted a rare thing or braw thing,
Ye had nae mair ado than clap on yer hat,
And awa to his shop, and that thing ye gat;
For a' thing he kept, and wi' that got the name—
'Twas aye Willie a' Thing, and will be the same.
In his day Galashiels was but a sma' toon,
And few braws frae Lon'on then ever came doon;
The staple commodity then was grey claith,
And maister and servant it clad them aye baith.
Though folk have despised it for mony lang years,
Yet, thanks for the taste o' our braw volunteers—
There's naething looks better than Galashiels
grey—
It haps the brave hearts now the toast o' the day.
Fewer wants the folk had in auld Willie's time,
And for what they did need his shop answer'd
prime.
He had flirds for the lassies, breeks for the men,
And cleadin' for bairns and folk three score and ten.
And a' kinds o' hardware he keepit forbye,
Frae lang-saws to needles, in endless supply.
The country folk dealt wi' him baith far and near,
And a' that they bought they ne'er thought was
owre dear;

And neither they could, for he wasna the man
That follow'd the rule, Take and grip a' ye can.
He was honest, and that is what I ca' nae sma'
       thing—
It was seen in the face aye o' guid Willie a' Thing.

An airy young blade came a'e day to our town,
Wha had heard about Willie's great shop o'
      renown.
He sune socht it out, wi' the brilliant intention
Of asking for something wad puzzle his gumption,
Make him search a' his shop for twa hours or
      three,
And make Willie a' Thing a' Naething to be.
So, entering at once, said, " I come here to buy
A pair of good handcuffs, pray can you supply ?"
Said Willie, " I'll see, ye had better step ben,
I'm sayin', I'm sayin', I'll sune let ye ken ; "
So, lookin' aboot for a minute or twa,
He added, " This day I'm sell'd out o' them a'
But I'll take yer measure, and ye'll ca' the morn"—
Syne pull'd out a cord and tied fast the greenhorn.
" I'm sayin', I'm sayin'," said Willie, " ye're fit—
Get oot at ma door"—so the biter was bit,
The Englified puddin'-pock had to retreat,
Handcuff'd like a criminal, out to the street.

       *   *   *   *   *   *

To scenes in years fled mem'ry oft wanders o'er—
I see a dense crowd yet, a' round Willie's door,
Wha bore him away to the Auld Toon Kirkyard,
And laid his auld head 'neath the green grassy
    sward.
The numbers that follow'd him to his lang hame
Exceed a' that's follow'd ane there ye could name.
Though then a bit callant, my heart it was sair
When I thought his kind looks I ne'er wad see
    mair.
Even wee toddlin' bairnies, wi' grief in ilk face,
Gazed lang doon the street when removed frae his
    place,
And told when they saw the black train move away,
"Willie a' Thing they'd put in a hole 'mang the
    clay."
And mony a ane has since then left the scene,
And now pass'd away as if they had ne'er been;
The auld funny jokers in youth whom we knew,
Are wearin' away too, and now gettin' few.
Yet some there are left; may each guid-hearted
    billie
Receive our respect to the end, like auld Willie.
Though lang he lived here, he's now like an awa
    thing—
For among things that were is now Willie a'
    Thing.

TO SUMMER.

BEAUTEOUS Summer! list my song,
Ere thy glories pass away.
I have loved thee, and would fain
Sing thy charms in artless lay;
Time proclaims through all our land,
Short, alas! must be thy stay.
With thy gorgeous train attending—
Fruits and flow'rs of every hue—
We have seen thee come, sweet smiling,
O'er the landscape stretch'd to view,
Strewing round thee choicest blessings,
Pleasures ever fresh and new.

Bounteous Summer! when the earth
Lay despoil'd, all bleak and bare,
Balmy odours didst thou breathe
O'er each dropping flow'ret there.
Forms of life and beauty sprang
Wanton 'neath thy fostering care.
Fields of corn around us waving
Glad our hearts, and bid us see
Selfishness is human nature—
God of Nature! none in thee

We can find; then, oh how grateful
Should thy thankless creatures be.

    Parting Summer! ere you fly,
    Bear upon thy silken wings
    Grateful homage, due to thee
    For a thousand nameless things:
    We have felt, but cannot tell
    Half the joy thy coming brings.
Other climes across the ocean
Wait thy coming, and the knell
Of departure now is ringing—
Rings, alas! to break the spell
That hath bound us to adore thee,
Smiling Summer, fare-thee-well!

——:o:——

A WISH.

(Written for an Album.)

May health and happiness be thine,
And may thy path through life still shine
    Without one cloud of sadness;
And when at last thy race is run,
Then calmly as the setting sun,
    Sink, but to rise in gladness.

SONNET.—TO MAY.

Come, smiling May, with all thy lovely train
  Of opening buds, and flow'rets fresh and fair,
  That shed their fragrance on the balmy air,
And breathe sweet kisses, through thy wide
    domain.
Now through the woods the vocal chorus rings,
  From all the warbling throng, at early morn;
  And measured notes from yonder straggling
    thorn
Hail thy approach, for hark! the cuckoo sings.
Delightful season! oft would I repair
  To the green hills beneath thy smiling skies,
  Where each low worldly care and passion dies,
Amid the tranquil scenes that soothe us there;
  The varied landscape stretching to the view,
  Disclosing charms, still rising ever new.

THE LUCKY NIGHT.

In rhyme I'll begin, and will try to narrate
A story quite true, as I heard it of late.
A rare ane it is, and ye'll say it's as queer
As ony ye've heard o' for mony a year.
It happen'd a'e nicht, down the country a wee
(But I'll no name the spot, for fear I may lee),
A strange lookin' blade, dress'd in shabby genteel,
Wha has lang roved the country, a puir ne'er-do-
    weel,
Was late on a harvest nicht rather hard set,
And stood lookin' thoughtfully o'er an auld yett.
His pouches were toom, and nae lodgings had he,
Nor kend where in sleep he had best close his e'e.
At last he resolved just to sleep 'mong the stooks,
And stole up the field wi' disconsolate looks.
The full moon was up, and the stars shining bright,
When he gather'd some sheaves for a bed thro'
    the night;
And lo! he espied there a dark lookin' figure—
And *darkey* it was, too, for he was a nigger—
Preparing his bed as the other had done;
And so the two met, and my story's begun.

The black seem'd a juggler, or mountebank loon,
Sic' as often we see in the streets o' our toon.
A trumpet hung danglin' down by his side,
For drawing the crowd when pursuing his trade.
That night he was hungry, and so was the other,
And soon they agreed they wad march on thegither
To the near farmhouse, just to get some repast
Before they lay down a' the night there to rest.
Human nature they studied while trudgin' alang,
And thought in the kitchen they couldna he
    wrang ;
There trust to the lassies their wants to supply,
As kind-hearted lassies can naething deny.
And rightly they guess'd, for we a' brawly ken
They want the rough feelings o' hard-hearted
    men.
But as for a supper they ne'er saw the sight,
For out stepp'd the farmer and carried a light ;
And a big bunch o' candles he carried forby.
And so when they saw him they never drew nigh,
But fled wi' a' speed to a wide open door,
And enter'd the barn, which was a' seated o'er.
The farmer he follow'd, but saw na' the pair,
As they sprung to the loft and took shelter there,
And peepin' out owre to see how things stood,
They saw the auld farmer in grave lookin' mood
Arrangin' and lightin' the candles in raws,
Stuck in turnips for need, and bereft o' the shaws.

Sane the folk gather'd in, and laid down their
    brass
In a plate that was set where the bodies did pass.
So the worthies abune now saw the thing clear,
They must patiently wait a sermon to hear—
Preach'd there for the purpose o' raising a fund
For building a schule-house new off at the grund.
A minister rose frae an auld arm-chair,
And open'd the meeting wi' praise and wi' prayer,
Then read frae the Bible the words here annexd—,
" Blow the trumpet, O Gabriel !" this was the text.
The nigger he grinn'd—raised his trumpet to
    blaw—
The other ane stopp'd him, and whisper'd him na,
Just wait till I tell ye, then blaw yer whole might,
And show yer black face, and we'll gie them a
    fright.
The minister spoke o' the use o' a trumpet;
For want o' a pulpit the table he thumpit—
He told how the high wa's o' Jericho fell,
And mair than a' that, had I time here to tell.
Explaining as lastly, wi' great animation,
The advantages gain'd thro' a guid education,
Then lustily bawl'd out the words o' the text—
" Blow the trumpet, O Gabriel !" Ah : what came
    next ?
A blast frae the nigger might waken'd the dead,
As he popp'd o'er the loft his black woolly head.

When they saw his grim visage look down frae
    the hole,
Superstition and terror appall'd every soul.
Some cried, 'twas the Devil; like drift out they
    flew,
While louder and louder the blackamoor blew,
And follow'd them out, while the other staid in,
Wha seized the collection, nor thought it a sin.
He handed the nigger twa shillings or three.
Bade him make an escape as hard's he could flee.
The knave wi' the rest fled a different way,
And slept 'mong the stooks till the first peep o'
    day,
Then forthwith he drew out his ill-gotten gear,
And counted out pounds up to twenty or near.
Few heard o' the splore, ilka ane there thought
    shame
The fright or the cause o't to mention or name—
They learn'd that the Devil frae whom they a'
    ran
Was nae deil ava, but a black nigger-man.
The rogue, some time after, wi' een sparklin'
    bright,
Told the tale o'er himsel' o' that "lucky night."

IN MEMORY OF BETSY DONALDSON
Who died at Walkerburn, 27th June, 1871.

——:o:——

Thou art gone to the grave and sadly we miss
    thee,
  But murmur we will not, nor dare to complain ;
For God, when he took thee, did only but bless
    thee,
  And our loss was only to thee future gain.

Sweet maiden ! thy short life's a true, simple
    lesson,
  That this world at most is a fast fleeting show;
And thy friends left bereaved, God loves, if he
    chasten,
  To wean them, like thee, from vain pleasures
    below.

When thy twin sister pined, care and grief
    gathered round thee,
  Thy young heart grew sick, and the dread
    spoiler came ;
But in calm resignation to God's will He found
    thee,
  And trusting in Jesus, and His holy name.

The grim king of terrors had nought to alarm
       thee,
   Through Faith, thy pale lips could exultingly
       sing—
My Saviour is with me, and He will disarm thee;
   O, Grave! where's thy victory! O, Death!
       where's thy sting?

For a short time, perchance, we may linger
       behind thee,
   On life's stormy ocean, to breast the wild wave,
But O! at the last, my soul, may death find thee;
   Like her's, fixed on One who is mighty to save.

Thou art gone to the grave, and we follow'd in
       sadness,
   And laid thee to slumber by Leithen's sweet
       stream;
Where again thou shalt rise in beauty and glad-
       ness,
   To find thy last hope here was no idle dream.

THOUGHTS ON THE BANKS OF GALA.

Is there a spot on earth more sweet
Than Gala's banks, where lovers meet
   At close of parting day;
Or, when the moon's unclouded beams
Are glitt'ring on the rocks and streams,
   Are nightly seen to stray ?

Thy rippling waters onward speed,
Through scenes of beauty, to the Tweed.
   By many a bush and tree,
That grace each brake and flow'ry dell,
To where they murmur fare-thee-well,
   By ancient Torwoodlee !

Haunts of my childhood ! whither fled
The early friends we hither led
   To pluck the choicest flowers,
Or chase the squirrel through the wood,
And watch them frisk in gayest mood
   Among the leafy bowers ?

Urged from their home and native land,
Perchance they form an exiled band
   On some far distant shore ;
Or, haply, reach'd that land of peace
Where friendship never more shall cease,
   And all their warfare o'er !

Hard is the fate, when sons of toil
Are forced to leave their native soil,
　　By threatening want oft driven;
O may they find, when life is o'er‘
A brighter and a happier shore—
　　A resting-place in heaven!

Is there a spot on earth so sweet
As that where weary pilgrims meet,
　　There never more to sever;
Nor care or sorrow ever know,
　　But, far beyond the reach of woe,
　　They live in bliss for ever ?

ACROSTIC.

M AY He who slumbers not nor sleeps,
A nd all his people safely keeps,
R emove all dangers, doubts, and fears;
Y ou guide, through many happy years.

W hile passing o'er life's thorny road,
A llay thy fears, still trust in God;
L et faith and patience bear thee through;
K now and believe thy Leader true.
E ternal joy, a crown of life,
R eward thee, Mary, dearest wife.

SONG.—WHAE'S LIKE MY AIN MARY?

Tune—"ROBIN ADAIR."

WHAE's like my ain Mary ?—
   Fair as the rose.
'Tis thy sweet smile, Mary—
   Soothes all my woes.
What were this world to me,
Mary, if wanting thee ?
Soon would I droop and dee—
   Sweet were life's close.

Fortune may frown, Mary,
   Favours depart,
But thou to me, Mary,
   More can impart ;
Give me thy look of love,
False tho' the world may prove.
Nothing can then remove
   Joy from my heart.

SCOTLAND'S HEATHER BELLS.

[Written on receiving some Sprigs from a Tourist, who plucked
them by the side of Loch Katrine.]

THOUGH others o'er the ocean wide
　To foreign lands may roam,
Yet Scotland ever still shall be
　My free and happy home.
I'll tune my harp, and touch the strings,
　For proud my bosom swells,
While musing on the upland scene
　Where bloom'd those heather bells.

Beside the fair Loch Katrine's brink,
　In summer's pride they grew;
And wet the hand that gather'd them
　With Scotland's mountain dew.
Though faded now their purple bloom,
　There's something left that tells
No sweeter flowers on earth are seen,
　Than Scotland's heather bells.

They deck the home of Freedom, where
　Fought many a noble band;
Where Bruce and Wallace martial strode,
　To guard our native land—
The land where martyrs bled and died,
　And many a hero dwells,

To strike a blow for Scotland yet,
  Among her heather bells.

Ye mountain cliffs, that proudly raise
  Your hoary heads on high,
Where lightnings play and eagles scream
  Beneath their native sky.
Below your cairns lie manly hearts,
  Nor time nor magic spells
Will e'er efface their memory,
  While bloom our heather bells.

Though far away in other lands,
  Scenes may lie bright and fair,
Yet give to me our heath'ry hills,
  For hallow'd haunts are there.
'Mid happy homes and joyous hearts,
  Is there a spot excels
The land where bright in beauty wave
  Our purple heather bells?

Old Scotland, where enthroned sublime
  Sweet Liberty is seen,
Where manhood walks unfetter'd still,
  And slave has never been—
Of thee I'll sing while life remains,
  Thy hills and lowland dells;
And bless thee while I wander free
  Among thy heather bells.

ACROSTIC.

W HEN first we met upon life's shifting scene,

I n boyhood then, and in experience green,

L ight were our hearts, I ween, and full of glee.

L o! what a change hath pass'd o'er you and me.

I nstead of fun and frolic, gloomy care

A ttends our steps, and follows everywhere,

M aking our raven locks now thin and bare.

F or years old Ocean hath between us roar'd;

R eturn'd again, and to thy friends restored,

A ccept, what honour, truth and friendship claim,

T his simple tribute, woven with thy name:

E ach earthly comfort cheer thee here below—

R ich and exhaustless may they ever flow.

SONG.—RIFLEMEN ARE FORMING.

Tune—" Draw the Sword, Scotland."

RIFLEMEN are forming! forming! forming!
Over all the Borders many a gallant band
Wait for the orders, the orders, the orders,
To repel the forces who dare invade the land.

The British banner, waving, waving, waving,
Shall ne'er be deserted by land or by sea,
But round it shall gather, gather, gather,
Each true-hearted son of the brave and the free.

Riflemen are forming, forming, forming,
When duty shall call them, with heart and with
    hand,
They will march to the onset, the onset, the onset,
And teach bold invaders the prowess of the land.

Riflemen are forming, forming, forming,
As rocks amid the tempest so firm they will stand,
And in the conflict, the conflict, the conflict,
Glorious deeds shall crown them, the heroes of
    the land.

Manly hearts are beating, beating, beating,
And yield they shall never, though cowards may
      fly,
They ne'er shall be conquer'd, conquer'd, conquer'd
For their Queen and country they will do or die.

Riflemen are forming, forming, forming,
In Britain's cause they rally—her freedom to
      defend;
And ours be the victory, the victory, the victory,
Over all the tyrants who dare invade the land.

———◦✕◦———

A NEW YEAR'S WISH.

TO LITTLE MARY.

As a young floweret, budding fair,
Opening its leaves in beauty rare,
     Sweet Mary, so art thou!
May no rude storms through life e'er blow,
To blanch thy cheek, nor grief e'er throw
     A shadow on thy brow.

May He who loves each little child
Still keep thee, darling, undefiled,
     From every taint below;
And grant thee many happy years,
'Till rais'd above earth's " vale of tears,"
     Where tears shall never flow.

EXCURSION TO PEEBLES.

ALONG the bonnie banks o' Tweed
　　'Twas lately, on a summer's day,
When off we went at railway speed
　　To see the Royal Burgh gay,

So leaving old St Ronan's Well,
　　And by the woods o' sweet Traquair,
We soon arrived at Peebles town—
　　That ancient town of beauty rare,

We quickly left the noisy cars,
　　And soon exchanged the stir and din
For softer seats and sweeter sounds,
　　Where glasses jingle at the inn.

Now ye who sign ' Permissive Bills,'
　　And judge men by their meat and drink,
Against a' Scripture, what care we
　　For what ye say, for what ye think ?

The Crown Hotel, 'twas there we met,
　　And drank to Peebleans, auld and young ;
Then sallied forth to see the town
　　O' which our auld King Jamie sung.

Here oft the Scottish monarchs came
 Langsyne, 'tis said, in merry mood,
Wi' high-born dames and gallants gay—
 A courtly train frae Holyrood.

And we suggest our gracious Queen,
 For auld langsyne, might here repair,
Without offence to northern friends.
 For pleasures new 'mid scenes so fair.

Ye fisher chiels that hither come
 For annual pastime and rare sport,
Here a' your wants can be supplied;
 To Stirling's shop at once resort.

There's rods, and reels, and fishing-lines;
 And hooks drest up, a' sorts and sizes;
And wading-boots, a' fishing gear—
 His catalogue ane quite surprises.

We met John Brunton, kind auld man,
 Wha showed us many a ferlie there;
Ilk scene o' beauty pointed out
 Makes famed auld Peebles everywhere.

We wandered to the auld kirkyard,
 Where mony a worthy Peeblean lies,
And read the records there that tell,
 In solemn words, Frail man he dies.

There Tait the bard has had his wish—
   That when his evening sun had set,
To mingle ashes 'neath the sward,
   Wi' worthies o' th' Auld Burgh yet.'

Rest, gentle bard, with those you lov'd :
   May no rude hand deface the stones
A loving daughter there has plac'd,
   To mark where rest thine honour'd bones.

To Neidpath Castle on we go,
   Grim and majestic there it stands,
As if in stern defiance yet
   Of Cromwell and his armed bands.

But all the clang of arms is hush'd,
   And nought is heard but Tweed's fair stream
Murmuring 'neath the battlements ,
   And all the past seems but a dream.

Oh ! Peebleshire thou'rt passing fair,
   This all confess when they behold thee,
But this sweet spot thy beauty crowns,
   And so in verse we have enroll'd thee.

On pleasure bent, we hither came
   To view thy varied scenes of beauty ,
Now having seen thee, we declare
   Each pleasure almost seems a duty.

Now for the rattling cars again—
  So, fare-thee-well, and Tweed's bright river;
Thy scenes by some may be forgot,
  But we'll remember thee for ever.

ACROSTIC.

G RATEFUL to thee, loved Minstrel of the Merse,
E ach day since first I read your pleasing verse,
O ft have I wish'd to pay this tribute due;
R eceive it then, for it belongs to you.
G enius and worth from me shall have their
    claim,
E ven an acrostic to thy honour'd name.

H eaven shower rich blessings as refreshing rains
E ach day on thee and thine, while life remains.
"N ature laments o'er all her beauties torn,"
D eath spare thee long, nor cause us so to mourn.
E steem'd by all, may friendship to the last
R eturn thee joys for cares and sorrows past.
S weet be life's close, when nobly thou hast
    striven,
O nward and upwards, may this hope be given,
N or given in vain—the blessed hope of Heaven.

THE AULD BEECH TREE.

O THE the sunny days of childhood, when, long,
    long ago,
We wander'd forth, a merry band, where wood-
    land flow'rets blow ;
And all the livelong summer's day, from care and
    sorrow free,
We sported round, or swung upon, the auld beech
    tree,

Engraven on its massive trunk familiar names I
    trace,
But what may be the features now of each fair
    blooming face ?
Will care and grief have alter'd them as they have
    alter'd me ?
Since here I sported with them round the auld
    beech tree.

Ah ! some have gone to other lands, and far across
    the deep,
While others in the auld kirkyard are laid in
    death's long sleep,
The joyous voices now are hush'd that often rang
    wi' glee,
While here in youth we sported round the auld
    beech tree.

As here I lonely turn again, and muse upon the
    past,
Sweet visions come as those in youth, but, ah!
    they cannot last ;
We feel the world is something else than what it
    seem'd to be,
When here in youth we sported round the auld
    beech tree.

When gazing o'er life's chequer'd scene of mingled
    joy and woe,
The world at best seems now to me a false and
    glittering show ;
And empty as the foambells seen upon a treach'-
    rous sea,
Seem now the hopes we cherish'd 'neath the auld
    beech tree.

Yet here I love to linger still, though life's young
    dream is o'er,
Its bright green leaves are fair to see as in the
    days of yore ;
And on its boughs the little birds sing sangs sae
    sweet to me,
That lang I gaze and listen 'neath the auld beech
    tree.

'Tis here I view the dear auld scenes that never
    tire the sight,

Where oft I stray'd with one I loved, fair as the
    queen of night—
That looking down has oft beheld, when no one
    else might see,
The trysts we set and kept beneath the auld beech
    tree.

How sweet to me the woodland scene, with leafy
    honours crown'd,
And nature's varied beauties spread in gay profu-
    sion round;
But from the fairest of them all I fondly turn
    mine e'e,
To yonder hallow'd spot, where stands the auld
    beech tree.

ACROSTIC

On receiving Verses containing beautiful Description of Flowers.

P LEASED, I read your beautiful song,

E very line to Nature is true,

T ouch by touch, you paint the gay throng—

E ach fairy-like flower as it grew.

R adiant they gleam in robes of light,

P eering forth with their starry eyes ;

A nd meet our gaze, all dazzling bright,

I n a thousand glorious dyes.

S weet may the season still return,

L aden to cheer life's latest hours !

E ven in age when frail and worn,

Y ielding thee joy, 'mong summer flowers.

IN MEMORY OF THE LATE REV. WM. DOBSON, INNERLEITHEN.

Winter is past, sweet Spring returns,
But ah! how many a bosom burns
In looking back, and sadly mourns
   Friends pass'd away,
And laid to moulder in the urns
   With kindred clay.

And thou, too, sainted one, art fled,
The sere leaves rustle o'er thy bed—
Thy lowly couch among the dead,
   By Leithen's stream.
Where rests thy weary, honour'd head
   From life's strange dream.

Thy kindly voice no more we'll hear
Pour comfort forth in sorrow's ear;
For with thine aid thou still wert near
   To the distrest,
Pointing to One who sojourned here
   To give them rest.

No more within the house of God
We'll hear thee teach the heavenward road,
Through One who bore the weighty load
   For sinners vile ;
And here endur'd the chastening rod,
    Though free from guile

Gifted with every Christian grace,
With heaven reflected in thy face,
Thy looks adorn'd the sacred place—
   The house of prayer ;
And time, we hope, will ne'er efface
    The truth's taught there.

Left in a world where friends are few,
Fond memory back would fain renew
Hours pass'd with those we no more view
   Again below ;
But ah ! vain thought, the picture's true—
    Earth's fleeting show.

Thou'rt gone, dear friend, for such thou wert—
Love to all men warm'd thy good heart,
Pure and unmix'd, no gloss of art
   Gilded it o'er ;
And Heaven's own love, thou hast thy part
    For evermore.

THE FAIRY DEAN.

COME to Allen's haunted stream,
Where its waters sparkle bright;
View with me the fairy scene
There, beneath the pale moonlight,
And amid the deep serene
At the witching hour of night!
Through the glen the rowing waters
Charm the air with music sweet
While their rippling crystal wavelets
Kiss the pebbles at our feet,
Lave the shore, and softly murmur,
Where the fays and fairies meet!

Further on we'll wander now
To the well-known Fairy dean;
Ample proofs are there to show
Where the tiny elves have been—
Where they led the mystic dance
Nightly on the dewy green.
Sights have here been seen and thrilling;
What has been may be again;
Fancy yet can paint them tripping,
Beings neither sprites nor men.

Dear are still our first emotions
In this haunted fairy glen!

Here in youth we often stray'd—
Spent the live-long summer day,
Gathering wondrous-looking toys
Fairy hands had done in clay,
While the merry tale went round,
Chasing all our fears away.
Calm retreat! where care and sorrow
Ne'er disturb'd our youthful dream,
How we love to muse and wander,
While our memory here doth teem
With returning joys of pastime
By this fairy haunted stream.

Now from Langshaw's ruin'd tower
Owlets screaming take their flight,
While the moonshine from on high
Gilds the scene with sacred light;
Winding waters, rocks, and trees
Rise conspicuous to the sight!
Charming scene of Nature's dressing,
All thy beauty who can tell?
Gazing here we fondly linger,
And reluctant sigh farewell
To thy haunts and sweet recesses,
Where the fays and fairies dwell!

SONNET.—TO JAMES HENDERSON, D.D.

[Written a short time before his death.]

Reverend Pastor, whom we all do love,
  As one long lent to guide us here below,
  And teach what God requires, and will bestow
On erring man, and has reserved above
For those who turn to Him, and live anew—
  Even chief of sinners, if no more they stray,
  But follow Jesus Christ, the living way,
And trust His finish'd work and mission true:
May He who led thee through, in days gone
    past,
  In thy declining years be with thee still,
And give thee strength, to stand forth to the
    last,
  An honour'd Watchman set on Zion hill;
And when at last thy Christian warfare's o'er,
A crown of life reward thee, evermore.

THE COMING NEW-YEAR.

HEAVY laden it comes, with joys and with
    sorrows,
With smiles and with tears hid in future to-
    morrows,
And we meet its approach in hope and in fear,
And wait the events of the coming New Year.

To the young and the gay it comes as a dream—
A vision of bliss upon life's sunny stream;
While with the smooth current they gaily career,
And hail with a welcome the coming New Year.

And who, with a heart, would e'er wish to
    destroy
The high hopes they cherish of sunshine and
    joy?
Their dark days of grief soon enough may be
    here,
To furrow each brow in the coming New Year.

To some it comes dark as a wave on the sea
Of the limitless ocean, Eternity;
On the voyage of life how many now steer
Will sink 'neath the wave in the coming New
    Year.

Heavy laden it comes, with sickness and pain,
As others before have again and again!

And maybe to snatch from us friends we hold
    dear,
And all that we love in the coming New Year.

When the winter is past, we know it will bring
The music of birds and the beautiful spring;
And sweet flowers of summer again will appear,
To deck out in beauty the coming New Year.

But ah! there are flowers that lie wither'd and
    dead,
It ne'er will restore from their cold narrow bed,
To comfort the mourners, whom nought else can
    cheer,
On life's dreary march in the coming New Year

Heavy laden it comes with thoughts of the
    tomb—
Of the great judgment day and man's final
    doom,
And bids us prepare, lest an hour, dark and
    drear,
May seal up our fate in the coming New Year.

Mysterious Time! on thy unfathom'd tide
How vacant we look, and how careless we
    glide;
God grant that his presence may ever be near,
To guide and protect through each coming New
    Year.

A C R O S T I C.

J OINT-STOCK of what on earth I hold most
    dear,

O n this first morning of another year,

H ere's to thee, friend, and do thou pledge the
    same,

N or scorn this simple tribute to thy name.

M ay years on years, successive as they flee

O ver thine head, still bring new joys to thee,

R iches, with honours, and a sweet wee wife,

R esolved to cheer and comfort thee through life.

I n peace and love, may all thy days run past,

S erenely bright, and joyous to the last—

O 'er all the ills of life, even to the end,

N obly may'st thou still rise, mine honour'd
    friend.

S O N G.

[As sung at the Celebration of Burns's Centenary in Galashiels,
25th January, 1859.]

Tune.—" Scots wha Hae," &c.

Let your banners proudly wave,
Scotia's sons, ye true and brave;
While the thistle decks his grave,
    Sacred be his memory

Who refuse at Burns's name,
All the honours it doth claim !
Let us boast his worth and fame
    Down to all posterity !

Men of Gala ! swell the strain
O'er the land, across the main !
Hail ! the day returns again—
    Celebrate his Centenary !

Be not mute amid the throng,
Sound his praises loud and long
Ye of his immortal song—
    The braw, braw lads of Gala !

May his lofty strains inspire
Britons yet to strike the lyre—
Draw from free-born son and sire
    Songs of love and liberty !

Scotia still shall drop a tear.
O'er her noble son so dear,
And with throbbing heart sincere
    View her minstrel's cemetery.

S O N N E T.

Dear Crawford ! may thy path through life
    prove sweet,
  In health, and happiness, may you be spared
  Through many coming years—thy good heart
    shared
In love to God and man, and to defeat
The various ills of life, that will retreat ;
  Such love can suffer much ; and will endure
  Throughout them all, while 'midst them pleas-
    ures pure
Will fall as sweetest flow'rets at thy feet,
'Till in a better world, earth's turmoil o'er—
  Again we'll meet, and there for ever be,
Where storms shall never beat, on that blest shore,
  The calm haven of a long eternity.
Such blessings then, dear friend, may they be thine
Is the fond wish and ardent prayer of mine.

TO A ROBIN.

WEE Robin Redbreast, sweet's thy sang,
Warblin' sae cheery a' day lang;
Nae ither bird, where'er we gang,
  Is heard but thee,
Though a' the wuds sae lately rang
  Wi' melody.

When autumn's north winds surly blaw,
And threaten us wi' frost and snaw,
Nae fear ye seem to hae ava
  O' hardships comin';
Philosophy ye teach us a'.
  Baith man and woman.

While we puir mortals fret and glow'r
Into the dark and future hour,
Until misfortunes seem to lour,
  Though nane are near,
A thrilling gush o' joy ye pour,
  Without a fear.

Nae doubt ye're an eccentric bird,
Singin' when nae ane else is heard—
Sae crousely, too; upon my word
  Ye're worth them a',
And bravely show ye're nae way fear'd
  For comin' snaw.

That ye're a tyrant some folks say,
And make o' other birds a prey ;
If true, what better, freend, are they ?
  Even their ain kind.
They've aye been kenn'd to rob and slay,
  Time out o' mind.

And then they boast superior sense ;
But, Robin, ye make nae pretence,
Even beasts and birds are oft a mense
  To mankind's race,
If at the world we take a glance
  Right face to face.

Langsyne, 'tis said, when in a wood
A cruel uncle, in cold blood,
Left the two children without food,
  To starve and die,
A Robin, like an angel good,
  Was hoverin' nigh.

And when in death they beauteous lay,
He gather'd leaves for many a day,
And strew'd them o'er, as I've heard say,
  In pious mood,
That children yet their homage pay
  To a' thy brood.

In winter, when the evening fire
Is stirr'd, and cheerful burns higher,
The listening wee folks round their sire
    Oft hear the tale,
And while kind Robin they admire,
    Sic pastime hail.

Though careless now ye sit and sing,
I fear, wee bird, ere comes the spring,
Around the doors, on shivering wing,
    Thou'lt chirp and flee;
Yet some thy look'd-for crumbs will bring,
    And strew for thee.

And how consoling 'tis for all,
That He who guides this earthen ball
Yet deigns to mark the sparrow's fall;
    So you and I,
On Him who hears ilk creature's call,
    May safe rely.

Sing on, blithe bird, I'll learn of thee
Still mair contented yet to be;
Life and its cares will quickly flee,
    It's nae use sobbin';
Henceforth I'll imitate thy glee—
    Adieu! Cock Robin.

LINES FOR THE SEASON.

DECEMBER 1857.

WHERE are thy young flowers,
 Beautiful May ?
Where are the loving hearts,
 Dearer than they ?
They are gone, cries a sad voice—
 They are not here ;
You might have spared them yet,
 Ruthless Old Year.

Are they for ever lost,
 Wither'd and dead ?
Shall they not spring again
 From their low bed ?
They shall live, cries a sweet voice—
 Softly but clear ;
Yes, when thou too art gone,
 Fleeting Old Year.

Long though their rest may be,
 Shrouded in clay,
That voice shall yet reach them—
 Call them away ;

Friends parted shall meet again,
This dries the tear,
Shed for those fled with thee—
Passing Old Year.

———••••••———

PLEASURES OF SPRING.

HARK! through the forest boughs,
And where the heather grows,
How the glad chorus doth echo and ring:
Winter is past and gone ;
Hush'd is the tempest's moan—
Nature exults in the pleasures of Spring.

Soft now the breezes blow,
Bright now the waters flow,
Through the green valleys they murmur and
sing;
There the wild flow'rets rise,
Open their starry eyes,
Bright with the beauty and glory of Spring.

Soon shall the flow'ry dells
Wave with their purple bells;

Then will the bee sip their sweets as they cling,
 And from each lovely breast,
 Where they shall softly rest,
Draw there with pleasure the blessings of Spring.

 Far in the sunny sky,
 Where fleecy clouds do lie,
Now springs the lark, waving joyous its wing,
 And at heaven's golden gate
 Sings to its loving mate,
Nestled below 'mong the blossoms of Spring.

 Through the stream's silver tide
 Finny tribes dart and glide,
Forming a pastime for peasant or king;
 Where they may pass the day,
 Chase all its cares away—
Calmly enjoy the rare sport of the Spring.

 Now let us forth and stray
 Where all is fresh and gay;
Sweet are the pleasures the season doth bring.
 Seek then the rural scene,
 And there in joy serene
Welcome the health-giving breezes of Spring.

SONNET.

[Written on viewing Floors Castle from the opposite side of
the Tweed.]

HAIL, beauteous spot! gem of our native isle,
　　Where once again my weary eye can rest,
　　And view thee now in all thy beauty drest,
Surpassing fair, 'neath summer's sweetest smile.
How oft would I life's anxious cares beguile,
　　And here repair when such disturb my breast—
　　A pleasure find 'mong beauties here confess'd,
Though home were distant from me many a mile.
Now on my listening ear comes music sweet,
　　From Tweed's bright waters rippling on with
　　　　speed.
To where the Teviot's silv'ry stream they meet—
　　There, blending down the vale, their course
　　　　they lead,
'Mid farewell murmurs to the distant sea,
And leave me fondly gazing still on thee !

NIGHT MUSINGS.

How calmly in the western sky
Now sinks the sun, 'mid rosy blushes;
At such an hour how sweet to lie
Listening where the water gushes!

Contrasted with the city's din,
Then, oh! how sweet to hear it brawling
Wild music o'er the craggy linn,
And see it foaming—ever falling!

And now it murmurs calm and slow,
Through the green valley softly gliding;
How passing sweet the moments flow,
While peace and love seem here presiding!

Hark! from the vale and through the trees
Comes music soft as infant sighing,
Or angel's whispers on the breeze
O'er a suffering saint when dying.

The shades of evening deepen now
O'er the fair landscape late so smiling;
As care and sorrow on the brow,
Where once sat joy, bright youth beguiling.

All Nature's hush'd, and now at rest,
Seems clothed as with a robe of sadness;
The lark hath sought her low-built nest,
And pours no more the tide of gladness.

Flowers disappear amid the gloom,
No longer now the fields adorning;
As flowers of life that in the tomb
Wait for a coming brighter morning.

'Tis but a night, a cheerless night,
And then the sleepers shall awaken,
Restored again to life and light;
They are not lost whom death has taken.

DARNICK BURN.

SWEET stream, where first in youth I stray'd,
Before my tongue could lisp thy name,
Though time hath wrought sad changes here,
Thou ripplest onward, still the same.
Where are my first companions now?
In vain I look, in vain I turn;
Their smiling faces now no more
Are seen to brighten Darnick Burn.

'Twas here I drew my infant breath,
In the sweet village by thy side;
Where stands the well-known tower and tree
Reflected in thy crystal tide.
Sweet are thy murmurs, gentle stream,
Tho' sighing here and doom'd to mourn
Departed joys with friends so dear,
As those I loved by Darnick Burn.

I love to see thee wimpling clear—
Thy verdant banks with gowans clad;
And still I love to linger near
With feelings pleased, tho' lone and sad.
But loving hearts are now away,
Cold lie their ashes in the urn,
Who cherish'd me in years long past,
And watch'd my steps by Darnick Burn.

Farewell then, gentle, rippling stream,
And smiling village, tower and tree,
Where joys return sweet as a dream
Of long-forgotten melody.
Where'er on earth I chance to roam,
Yet here at last would I return,
Here end my life where it began,
Amid the scenes by Darnick Burn.

VERSES TO TIBBIE SHIEL

"' 'What's Yarrow but a river bare?'
  Said Wordsworth, that purr peevish chiel';
I trow he'd found nae bareness there,
  Had he but kent kind Tibbie Shiel."
                              HENRY SANDERSON.

TIBBIE, ye're a witchin woman—
  A' our poets sing o' thee—
To the lochs some day I'm comin',
  Then your bonnie face I'll see.

In my time I've seen rare lassies—
  Lassies bonnie, trig, and braw;
Your description far surpasses
  Ony that I ever saw.

Whiles a flower they hae ye paintit,
  Whiles a fairy on the green—
A' sic stuff as that they've rantit—
  Maybe ye're the Fairy Queen.

That there have been elves and fairies,
  Hogg could whiles hae gien his aith,
When he wander'd by St Mary's,
  'Mid the scenes that nursed sic faith.

Oft he saw their moonlit capers,
  If what a' is said be true,
Clad in green wi' mouse-skin slippers,
  Sipping pearly draps o' dew,

When I'm in your fairy land,
  Guidsake Tibbie, treat me richt;
Keep in check the elfin band,
  I may dee wi' perfect fricht.

I'm thinkin' folk are whiles mista'en—
  See nae fairies when they ca';
And when they find ye just alane,
  Ye maun answer for them a'.

While's ye'll think folks lost their reason;
  Jamie Hogg's to blame for't a'.
Bringin' fools on you ilk season,
  Seekin' fairy folks sae sma.'

He was like nae ither being;
  When he met a bonnie lass,
Then it's clear and easy seeing
  For a fairy she wad pass.

Hogg in dreamy speculation
  Lived, nor saw things as they were,
So wi' little calculation
  We can see how he might err.

Ance he thought to ride a comet,
  Plough the moon and stars aside—
Even the apostles o' Mahomet
  Never thought o' sic a ride.

Nane could write sic queer auld stories,
  Ower them a' he bore the gree;
He's awa wi' a his nories,
  Peace be to his memory,

Ne'er was shepherd lad sae giftit:
  Whae could sing sae sweet a strain?
And his harp, say, whae can lift it,
  Tune its silent strings again?

May the stane that's been ereckit
  Keep in mind our shepherd bard,
And beside it loved, respeckit,
  Tibbie, may ye lang be spared.

Fare-ye-weel then, dearest Tibbie,
  Happy may ye live and dee;
May the magic o' a nibbie
  Keep ilk loon frae harmin' thee.

IN MEMORY OF ADAM WALKER.

Who Died at Innerleithen, 19th Nov. 1878.

AULD social freend ; thou'rt noo awa,
And left thy shopmates ane an' a ;
Succumb'd at last to nature's law
   And common doom,
Thy shuttles never mair to thraw
   Across the loom.

Here thirty years, at steady pace,
Ye sent them through thy auld loom's race,
Oft turning roond thy cheery face
   To see them speed ;
Alas ! another's ta'en thy place,
   For thou art dead.

Thy Leithen friends now miss thee sair—
Thy cheery smile they'll ne'er see mair ;
Thy wit and humour—rich and rare—
   Is at an end,
That often lightened toil and care—
   Dear honoured friend !

Thy native Peebleans, far and near,
Heard the sad tale wi' mony a tear
When the auld friend they lo'ed sae dear
   Was ta'en awa';
That weekly came for mony a year
   To see them a'.

'Tis nae poetic stretch to say
The little birds on every spray
Will miss thee now, upon thy way
   To Peebles toon,
And sing, methinks, in strains less gay
   When spring comes roon'.

So fancy speaks; but in our ear
There comes a truth baith sweet and clear—
That in a brighter, nobler sphere.
   When life is o'er,
Again we'll meet wi' friends held dear,
   To part no more.

Farewell, dear friend! Thou'rt now at rest
'Mong other worthies o' the past
In the kirkyard ye lo'ed the best,
   By Tweed's fair stream ;
In the " Auld Burgh " free at last
   From life's strange dream.

SONNET.—TO ASHIESTIEL.

HAIL! ye sweet sylvan scenes, so charming fair,
  In peace may honour'd worth there still preside,
  And pleasures flow, pure as the silv'ry tide
That laves thy flowery banks, and murmurs there
Sweet as the music floating through the wood,
  From warbling birds on each fair spreading tree,
  That offer up their songs to Heaven and thee,
And rear amid thy bowers their tender brood.
Along thy shaded walks, in joy serene,
  Long may the family band be seen to stray,
Blending their presence with the woodland
      scene,
  Heaven for their guard by night, their guide by
      day.
At summer's eve oft would I stray, and feel
The joy thy scenes impart, fair Ashiestiel!

M A Y.

"Woods and groves are of thy dressing;
 Hill and dale doth boast thy blessing."—MILTON.

'TIS now the merry month of May—
Come to the woodlands, come away.
Where the first flowers of summer blow,
And sparkling waters sweetly flow,
To where the soft and balmy breeze
Sighs through the blossom-laden trees;
There we can wander and enjoy
Serene delight without annoy.

Now the gay lark is soaring high,
And far up in the sunny sky,
To where the fleecy cloudlets rest,
And where it heaves its joyful breast,
Warbling sweet strains, so full and free,
As if from heaven the melody.
And now the sun's bright golden beams
Are glowing on the crystal streams;
The bees are humming, birds are singing,
And all the woods with music ringing,
To call you forth without delay,
And pass a summer's holiday.

Freed from the crowded city's din—
With peace without and peace within—
How sweet on some green spot to lie,
Beneath the smiling summer sky;
Or on some neighbouring height to stray,
And watch the lambkins as they play—
There list the music of the rill
Murmuring down the verdant hill,
To meet the waters as they flow
Through the fair smiling scene below;
Winding their course by bush and tree,
Far to the bosom of the sea.
Along their banks, so cool and green,
There men and maidens fair are seen;
The angler with his rod in hand,
To draw his finny tribe to land;
The milk-maid, in the grassy mead,
Where lowing cattle stray and feed;
The shepherd, with his crook and plaid,
Reclining 'neath the hawthorn shade;
The shelter'd cot beside the wood,
And children there in gayest mood;
All sporting round the old oak tree,
In innocence right merrily.

Thus through the livelong summer day
All nature now looks fresh and gay;
And at mild eve, when in the west

The glorious sun slow sinks to rest,
His parting smiles now richer glow
O'er the fair landscape stretch'd below;
While hill and valley blushing stand,
Like some enchanted fairy land,
And clothed in beauty, own the sway
Of summer's queen—the Month of May.

Fair nature's smiling face come view,
With charms still rising ever new ;
Now in the rosy month of glee.
Of beauty, love and jollity,
When all we see, and all we hear,
Has power to charm the eye, the ear,
And smooth the way through care and strife,
Along the rugged path of life—
'Mid scenes which can pure joys impart,
And please the fancy, cheer the heart—
Come to the woodlands, come away,
And pass a summer's holiday.

THE BANKS O' GALA WATER.

Tune—" THE LASS O' GOWRIE."

AE summer night, at gloaming grey,
Across the muir I took my way,
To meet a lassie sweet and gay,
    On the bank o' Gala Water.

I met her where the sparkling tide
By Torwoodlee is seen to glide,
And drooping birks weep by its side,
    On the banks o' Gala Water.

The mavis raised its evening sang,
As hand in hand we stray'd alang,
And sweet the wuds wi' echo rang,
    On the banks o' Gala Water.

There, perch'd upon the highest tree,
A happy bird, nae doubt, was he;
But happier far, I trow, were we ,
    On the banks o' Gala Water.

Beneath the hawthorn's flowery shade,
I row'd her i' my guid grey plaid,
And a' my love was there repaid,
    On the banks o' Gala Water.

We wander'd till the moon shone bright,
And shed o'er a' her silver light;
And aye I'll mind that happy night,
    On the banks o' Gala Water.

'Twas there, wi' sma' persuasive art,
I won her warm and loving heart,
And vow'd frae her I ne'er would part,
    On the banks o' Gala Water.

And now she is my wedded wife,
Where, free frae worldly care and strife,
We live a sweet, contented life,
    On the banks o' Gala Water.

SONG.—MY MAGGIE AND ME.

WHEN sweet fa's the e'ening, O gie me the hour
To wander, dear lassie, within yon green bower,
Thy hand lock'd in mine, while the mavis sings
      free
In the woods o' Traquair, to my Maggie and me.

When the sweet flowers around us hae faulded
      their leaves
Around ilk fair bosom, my fancy conceives
If their wee hearts can love, nae purer they'll be
Than the twa loving hearts o' my Maggie and
      me.

When Tweed's gentle murmurs fa' soft on mine
      ear,
And the bright stars abune us begin to appear,
Mair sweet than Tweed's murmurs, or heaven's
      blue e'e,
Are the whispers and glances my Maggie gies me.

Fair scene o' endearment! wherever I go,
O, what sweeter bliss has this earth to bestow
Than to meet by Traquair, 'neath the auld
  trysting tree,
That screens wi' its green leaves my Maggie and
  me.

Ye winds softly sighing thro' Tweed's flowery
  vale,
O speak not our whispers nor tell our love tale ;
And Tweed's flowing river—go ! kiss the salt sea,
But leave the sweet kisses my Maggie gie's me.

Ye woods o' Traquair, ever dear to my heart,
If ever from thee I am forced to depart,
I ne'er will forget, till the day that I dee,
The hours we hae spent there, my Maggie and me.

TO A BEREAVED FRIEND.

CALM thy sorrows, smooth thy brow,
    Dry the tears of sadness;
Trials here, though grievous now,
    End in joy and gladness.

Sunshine follows shades of night,
    Through the woodlands glancing;
Clothing all in robes of light,
    Beautiful, entrancing.

Youth and beauty fade and die,
    Flowers of life are taken
Ransom'd spirits to the sky,
    Yet we feel forsaken.

Mariner on life's rough sea,
    O'er the waters bounding,
Peaceful shores are waiting thee,
    Parted friends surrounding.

Life is but a chequer'd scene,
    Joy and grief are blending;
Hope for heaven with soul serene,
    Bliss there never ending.

From sweet voices utt'ring joy,
  Hark! the music sounding;
Praise to God is their employ,
  Evermore resounding.

Calm thy sorrows, smooth thy brow,
  Dry the tears of sadness;
Trials here, though grievous now,
  End in joy and gladness.

THE AULD WITHER'D STUMP BY THE SIDE O' THE BURN.

WHERE now is the tree, wi' its green leaves ance
    waving ?
Again I revisit the sweet flowing stream,
That mirror'd its beauty, beneath it bright laving,
Langsyne, when I gazed here in childhood's young
    dream.
A' its wide spreading branches and leaves are
    away,
And nought of its beauty I see on return;
Though 'tis summer, it stands 'mid the beauties
    of May
An auld wither'd stump by the side o' the burn.

How sweet was the time, when in boyhood we
    wander'd !
A frolicsome band here, to pu' the wild flow'rs,
Or sit 'neath its shade, while the stream it mean-
    der'd,
And gleam'd in the sunshine of summer's bright
    hours.

Oft, along the green banks, mem'ry brings in
    array
The youthful companions, whose absence I mourn;
But alas! they are fled, I but see in decay
The auld wither'd stump by the side o' the burn.

'Tis summer, and sweetly the wild flow'rs are
    springing,
Again fair as ever are a' things we see,
But the auld wither'd stump, wi' roots to earth
    clinging,'·
As an earth-born mortal, till death sets him free.
Now amid the fair scene, where ance it stood
    fairest,
I leave it, and sigh for its beauty a' torn,
Nor will I forget it, 'mong flowers here the
    rarest—
The auld wither'd stump by the side o' the burn.

VERSES.

On seeing posted up within the walls of a Churchyard the
Notice, "No begging allowed," &c.

HERE often has the passing stranger gazed
On the strange "Notice" witty heads have raised,
To mock the honour'd dead, as one may guess,
And weary, wandering beggars as they pass.

Nay, rest in peace, they'll beg of you no more,
Though once they stood as suppliants at your door.
Nor need they to be told, that 'tis in vain;
A beggar here would surely be insane.

There's nought that you possess they e'er will crave,
The poorest wretch gets all you have, a grave,
The rich obtain no more, save at their head
A stone, to tell some happy heirs they're dead.

Go, naked, shivering beggar, trudge along,
Nor think that right ne'er triumphs over wrong,
For they who spurn you here from house and
    home,
May beg of you, as Dives, in time to come.

IN MEMORY OF LITTLE MARY.

WITH flowers of summer thou art gone;
 Ah! sweet wee Mary, thou art dead;
The autumn winds now sigh and moan
 Over the turf that wraps thy head.

We miss thee now among the throng
 Of happy children at their play;
And when they join in merry song,
 We think of Mary pass'd away.

We saw thee when thy face shone bright,
 And rosy health sat smiling there,
Nor thought that death so soon would blight
 A flower like thee, so young and fair.

But sweetest flowers must fade and die,
 And thou, alas! hast shared their doom,
Whilst we could only gaze and sigh,
 And lay thee in the narrow tomb.

Sweet voyager! thy journey's o'er,
   Thou'rt safe from every storm that blows,
And pain and sickness nevermore
   Can e'er disturb thy deep repose.

Thy little bark has reached the shore,
   And left us struggling far behind,
Sad, worn, and weary at the oar,
   Against each furious adverse wind.

Thou'rt gone, and would we wish thee here
   Again, upon life's troubled sea?
No, rather would we wish to steer
   To the calm haven that harbours thee.

For such as thee, snatch'd from our sight,
   To us is consolation given,
Since death was but thy spirit's flight,
   From cares of earth, to joys of heaven.

VERSES TO THE "GUID FOLKS" OF
S—— L——.

[Written in 1862, on reviewing the proceedings at that time
against a worthy Minister in the Parish of G———s The
distrust shewn, the false accusations brought against him,
and, besides, the low means used to effect the purpose of
his accusers, were, what the Author thought, an insult to a
people who have so long he'd him in high respect as their
faithful Minister.]

FAIR Charity, of heavenly birth!
If thou art still upon the earth,
Go visit S—— L—— in a dearth,
    Where souls are starvin';
The fare's but puir, and little worth,
    When Satan's carvin'.

Their evil hearts black thoughts engender,
Their tongues, unbridled, utter slander;
And charity, they never kenn'd her,
    Nor saw her face—
And yet, forsooth! they think to wander
    The Christian race.

Religion there is low indeed,
While a' that's bad reigns in its stead,

Foul slander foremost takes the lead
    To blast a name
As yet unstain'd, and wholly freed
    From aught of blame.

Their hearts seem poison'd black wi' sin;
Surcharged, the venom from within
Comes spewin' out 'gainst Mr P———n,
    A lava tide,
As if Vesuvius wi' its din
    Had open'd wide.

Some agents, here sent by the devil,
Came round wi' words sae sly and civil,
To note what they could hear o' evil,
    To bring him scaith;
As if folk here were on a level
    Wi' folk o' L———h.

"Auld Nick," nae doot ye thought if he
Came yonder, ye wad need to flee;
And so ye sent yer tools sae slee
    To do yer wark,
Lest ye should lose supremacy
    I' that same kirk.

If patronage they dinna like,
They needna be in sic a fyke,

Let them at anee just loup the dyke,
    Out o' the fold,
Or seek, like bees, some other byke,
    As they of old.

Even for eight hunder pounds a-year,
Sic awkward sheep I wadna wear;
The rot's among them there, I fear,
    Or something waur,
Defying a' that herds can smear
    In shape o' tar.

To style them sheep sounds rather fine,
As a comparison, say swine ;
'Tis written in the Book divine,
    And aptly penn'd,
" Cast not your pearls 'mong sic, lest syne
    They turn and rend."

The Scriptures stand for ever true,
And when the case we clearly view,
We see a pearl's been cast to you,
    Where ilka sumph
Turns round, among the swinish crew,
    Wi' angry grumph.

'Twere waste o' words, and waste o' time,
Else, would I spin a lengthen'd rhyme,

And make the verses sweetly chime.
    To sing the praise
O' him, whae's taught sic truths sublime
    'Maist a' his days

They who best know him, best can tell
He has discharged his duties well,
And a' the powers o' earth and hell
    He needna fear;
He whom he serves reward him shall,
    Ilk future year.

SONNET.—TO THE MOON.

To thee I lift mine eyes, thou lovely Moon!
  Sailing, majestic as the queen of night,
  And while I gaze upon thy holy light,
Grateful to Heaven, I hail the sacred boon.
More sweet than even the glorious Sun at noon
  Thou art, fair moon, as o'er a sleeping world
  Thy banner seems in love and peace unfurl'd,
Which morn, alas! will shrivel up too soon;
For with the morn return life's anxious cares,
  And weary toils, that wear that life away.
A banquet now indeed the poor man fares,
  He knows not of, .when shines the orb of day,
And many a weary sleeper soon shall rise,
To bless thy reign, fair empress of the skies!

VERSES.

Recited on the presentation of a Silver Cup to Mr JAMES
DALZIEL, by his EMPLOYEES, on his leaving Galashiels
for Walkerburn, Dec. 31, 1862.

How sweet to feel an all-wise plan
Is so arranged, that erring man
    Finds pleasure mix'd with duty;
For honour given where honour's due
Is duty, and a pleasure too,
    Besides a thing of beauty.

And so we feel when met to-night,
Where happy hearts and faces bright
    Are smiling all around us,
To give that honour due to one,
Before the year its course has run,
    As duty's call hath bound us.

No hard taskmaster e'er was he
Whom we thus honour, nor will be,
    He owns a higher nature,
Nor needs the boast of noble blood,
To make him either wise or good,
    Or measure out his stature.

And all now present here can tell
They ever found in James Dalziel
  A kind and generous master.
Would some but imitate his plan,
They'd find who in their service ran,
  To serve them, would run faster.

A modest youth he first came here,
And ever since hath his career
  With blessings been attended;
And Galashiels will find that day,
That sees him from us move away,
  A breach not easily mended.

But, as the Fates will have it so,
May our best wishes with him go,
  And happiness surround him,
May they of Walkerburn still find
A master generous, good, and kind,
  As we have ever found him.

The inscription graven on that cup
Shall oft be read, and it fill'd up,
  When friends around him gather;
And when long years have pass'd away,
May children's children proudly say—
  Such honour had our father!

MUSINGS FROM ST RONAN'S WELL.

Musing I sat by old St Ronan's well,
 Where Scott and Hogg and Wilson oft have
   been;
And many illustrious names the records tell
 Of those allured to this fair charming scene.

Embower'd 'mid evergreens, with fruits and
   flowers
 And warbling birds on every blooming spray
How sweet it is to pass the jocund hours
 That fleet so fast in summer time away.

The sparkling waters here are quaff'd the while
 For health and healing virtue in them lies,
And faces wan have here been made to smile,
 And drooping spirits often made to rise.

Down through the vale the Leithen waters glide
 To meet below fair Tweed's majestic stream;
The verdant banks are fringed on either side
 With foliage surpassing artist's dream.

Viewed from the neighbouring hill—sweet
    Caerlee hill,
  Lo ! what a glorious prospect meets the sight ;
The winding river fed by many a rill,
  Far as the eye can reach 'mid sunshine bright.

No wrangling sects or priestcraft here we need
  To tell our Maker's goodness there doth shine—
No Calvinistic doctrines there that lead
  To doubt or dread the Architect divine.

Each singing bird around us here doth preach,
  " O ye of little faith" who doubt, and pray,
Nature through all her works, more truth can
    teach
  Than aught that creed-bound teachers e'er
    convey.

Alas ! that truth in semblance should be sold
  As merchandise within the temple still—
That man will worship, yet, the calf of gold
  But Mammon leads them captive at his will.

Go silly dupes, and follow if you please
  The knaves who torture truth throughout the
    world ;
Happy the man who here can sit at ease,
  And see it clearly, all around unfurl'd.

     *   *   *   *   *   *

Amid this tranquil scene what thoughts arise,
　　While looking back and musing on the past,
Of many a friend we loved that lowly lies
　　At rest in yonder old churchyard at last.

And there the well known schoolhouse stands in
　　　　view,
　　Where early friends have met, and left the
　　　　scene;
Where are they now, the uproarious merry crew,
　　Who fought, or sported on the village green?

Mix'd in the busy throng of human life,
　　May fortune smile on them, by land or sea;
And through this changing scene of care and
　　　　strife,
　　Rich blessings on them, wheresoe'er they be.

Farewell thou beauteous scene and calm retreat,
　　Where love and peace, in union seem to dwell:
And never till fond hearts must cease to beat,
　　Shall be forgot, thy charms, St Ronan's Well.

SONG.—BONNIE LEITHEN SIDE.

AGAIN, sweet spring comes smiling forth,
   To chase the gloom away,
That dreary winter from the north
   Hath shed o'er bank and brae.
Then meet me charmer, ever dear,
   Thy footsteps let me guide,
Where all around combines to cheer,
   By bonnie Leithen side.

I'll lead thee where the winding stream
   So sweetly murmurs by,
No cares shall cloud love's golden dream,
   When thou, my love, art nigh.
And when the sun sinks in the west,
   The lovely moon will glide,
To gild thy way through scenes the best,
   By bonnie Leithen side.

And there I'll tell the tale of love,
   Which no one else may hear
But some sweet, gentle powers above,
   That know my words sincere.
And there I'll woo thy bonnie sel',
   To be my darling bride,
Till crowned with love and joy we dwell,
   By bonnie Leithen side.

SONG.—THE LASSIE O' CAULD HAME.

ALTHOUGH they ca' the place Cauld Hame,
  'Tis nae cauld hame to me;
It sets my heart a' in a flame,
  Ilk time that spot I see.
For there, a lassie lives, I trow,
  I needna tell her name,
I'll love, while Leithen waters row
  Sae sweetly by Cauld Hame.

On Leithen's banks lives mony a lass,
  And some may think them fair,
But nane, as far as I can guess,
  Wi' her will e'er compare.
And if I lo'e her 'bune them a',
  How can I be to blame,
She's stown my very heart awa'
  The lassie o' Cauld Hame.

Ae night I strayed o'er Caerlee hill,
  To view the scene below,
And thought if a' were at my will,
  The landscape could bestow,

I'd think the whole a paltry prize,
    Unless that I could claim,
The dearest treasure 'neath the skies,
    The lassie o' Cauld Hame.

But, in a little cot ere lang,
    Where Leithen waters glide,
I'll sing o' her a sweeter sang,
    When there she is my bride.
And though this meet wi' cauld disdain,
    O what care I for fame,
If ane will but approve the strain,
    The lassie o' Cauld Hame.

GILFILLAN O' DUNDEE.

[This appeared in the Dundee Weekly paper some years ago,
when the "Heresy hunt," as it has been called, was started.
The first intended victim was the late Rev. George Gilfillan,
and he gave full permission for its insertion.]

A brave, brave man Gilfillan was,
  And so at least, thought we,
When no langsyne, the bold divine,
  Spoke out so frank, and free ;
But now, Sir, ye have changed your tune,
  And back again to the auld croon ;
The Presbytery now craws abune
    Gilfillan o' Dundee.

On "Modern Heroes" ye may write,
  Or aught else till ye dee,
But keep frae scaith, some points o' faith,
  For ever let them be.
In Sion, sit just at your ease,
  Nor, like the pilgrim walk on peas,
Even hint that a' ye said were lees,
    Gilfillan o' Dundee.

And preach the gospel as ye like,
   But dinna preach it free ;
Be sure and tell that there's a hell,
   Some needna try to flee ;
For in the "Standards" they will find
   A certain number o' mankind,
For hell were born, for hell designed,
     Gilfillan o' Dundee.

And fish for D.D. to your name,
   Take this advice frae me ;
'Tis like the curl on a pig's tail,
   A pleasant sight to see ;
Then, like your freend in " Reekie's " toon,
   In vanity strut up and doon ;
The folk will press to touch your gown,
     Gilfillan o' Dundee.

The worship o' the "golden calf"
   Has been, and still shall be,
The only ane, to which some priests
   Delight to bend the knee ;
The calf's the god that blinds the eyes,
   O' him that sells and him that buys;
Mind this, and in the kirk ye'll rise
     Gilfillan o' Dundee.

And now ae word, and then I'm dune—
　　It sadly vexes me,
To think ye're settled down again,
　　Where nae guid man should be;
Where ye maun sit for ever dumb,
　　Or auld erroneous nonsense hum;
Out from amongst them, boldly come,
　　Gilfillan o' Dundee.

SONG.

Respectfully inscribed to the OPERATIVES OF BUCKHOLM MILL, as written for, and sung at, their Old Year Night's Entertainment.

COME, join in the chorus, huzza! huzza!
A new year is coming, huzza! huzza!
Though the auld ane elope, the new ane we hope
Comes wi' happiness sune to us a', us a'.

May it bring to us health, may it bring to us
      wealth,
That fu' canty and crouse we may craw, may
      craw ;
Should misfortunes e'er lour, may joys the next
      hour
Chase the dark clouds o' sorrow awa, awa.
            Come, join in the chorus, &c.

Our maidens sae sweet, and our lads trig and neat,
A' met here to trip through the ha', the ha',
Is a scene bright and fair, will make auld canker'd
      care
Think there's nae room for him here ava, ava.
            Come, join in the chorus, &c.

In our steady-gaun mill at the foot o' the hill,
Where Gala's sweet waters do fa', do fa',
Frae morning till e'en, sae eydent we've been,
Nae wonder we've met here sae braw, sae braw.
          Come, join in the chorus, &c.

To toast Buckholm Mill, a bumper we'll fill,
And rise to our feet in a raw, a raw;
That her trade may increase, and flourish in peace
Is the toast here to-night, then huzza! huzza!

Come join in the chorus, huzza! huzza!
A new year is coming, huzza! huzza!
Though the auld ane elope, the new ane we hope
Comes wi' happiness sune to us a', us a'.

EPISTLE TO A LADY BEFORE MARRIAGE.

MADAM, unskilful though I sing,
Yet once again I'll touch the string,
And from my harp will strive to bring
    For thee a strain,
Even though my muse may droop her wing,
    Nor sing again.

We hail'd the morn that gave thee birth,
And brought thee to the well-known hearth,
That waits again thy modest worth
    There to preside ;
And thy return, 'mid joy and mirth,
    We hail, sweet bride !

When comes the joyous bridal day,
The western breezes o'er Lea-brae
Will seem to mourn a flower away,
    When thou art gone,
And through the trees, as in dismay,
    Will sigh and moan.

The little birds, now warbling free,
Will seem to chirp from tree to tree ;
And chant their farewell notes to thee,
    In mournful mood,

And restless 'mong the branches flee
    Throughout the wood.

But joy be with thee and thy mate,
May love increasing bless thy state;
Nor strife, nor jealousy, nor hate
    To thee come nigh,
And may thy dwelling be the seat
    They ever fly.

May life's dark shadows never lour
O'er thee and thine, but may each hour
In bright succession glide, and shower
    All that is choice—
While blithe as birds in summer bower
    Your hearts rejoice.

Sweet modest maiden, young and fair!
If aught avails our fervent prayer,
Our words shall not be lost in air,
    But reach above,
And claim for thee Heaven's special care
    And watchful love.

May He who guides this earthen ball,
And deigns to mark the sparrow's fall,
Give comforts neither few nor small
    To thee through life,
And crown thee with our wishes all—
    A happy wife.

STANZAS.

Soft be thy slumbers, hapless one,
  Here in thy lone and narrow bed;
Though brief thy days, yet few or none
  Knew half the woes that bow'd thy head.

Now cold in death, almost forgot—
  Thy gay companions passing by
In careless haste, scarce mark the spot,
  Where youth and beauty ruin'd lie.

Thy sylph-like form, at summer's eve,
  No more by yonder trysting tree
Shall meet with him who could deceive,
  Though sworn to love, and live for thee.

Fair as a flow'ret was thy form,
  Seen bending 'neath the chilling blast,
And now the demon of the storm
  Laughs at the ruin o'er thee cast.

And he who could have saved thy life
  Now mixes with the giddy throng,
And bawls, 'mid revelry and strife,
  The obscene jest and wanton song.

Go, villain! laugh the hours away,
  And drown remorse with maddening wine!
But know, there comes a judgment day,
  To give account for deeds like thine.

Yes! she who now lies cold in clay,
  Will one day stand reveal'd to thee,
When thou shalt view her with dismay—
  A witness of thy perjury.

Come, gentle dews, and here distil
  Your pearly drops o'er her lone grave,
And come, ye winds that sweep the hill,
  To wipe them as ye howl and rave.

Thus mimic woe shame hearts so cold,
  Which cannot heave a sigh for one
Whose tale of grief can ne'er be told—
  Who loved too well, and was undone.

Ah! pity here might drop a tear
  O'er one so young, so early lost;
For joyless was her brief career,
  Ere death's dark stream she sadly cross'd.

Hark! on the breeze methinks I hear
  Her gentle spirit softly sigh—
"For me let no one drop a tear,
  Nor mourn for one who wish'd to die.

SONG.

" What is there in this world below
　　But disappointment, care and gloom:
There's nought but mercy in the blow
　　That lays the wretched in the tomb.

" My broken heart is now at rest,
　　And all my folly is forgiven;
My once sad spirit now is blest—
　　My home for ever is in heaven."

SONG.

Can I forget where last we met
  By yonder rippling crystal stream?
And thought the sun too soon had set,
  Which closed that day's delightful dream.

Ah no! those scenes I'll ne'er forget,
  The flow'ry banks, the leafy bow'rs;
The trysting place where last we met
  And spent the fleeting happy hours.

When through the wood sweet music rang
  Frae warbling birds on ilka tree,
I thought that love was a' their sang,
  Sweet lassie, when I roved wi' thee.

But now the birds hae changed their sang,
  And seem to chirp frae tree to tree;
And a' looks sad where'er I gang,
  For her I never mair shall see.

Fate urged her from me far away
  To other lands across the sea,
Where now she sleeps beneath the clay,
  While here I'm left to droop and dee.

Still 'mid those scenes I'll pensive stray
  Till death shall close my wat'ry e'e;
Though nature's face there still looks gay,
  Her fairest scenes seem blank to me.

NEW YEAR'S HYMN.

FOR SABBATH SCHOOLS.

A song of praise, O Lord, to Thee,
  A New Year bids us sing;
And gratitude our theme shall be,
  Before the Lord our King.

Thus far, as pilgrims on the road,
  In mercy we've been spar'd;
And all our cares and wants, O God,
  Have met Thy kind regard.

Our teachers do Thou bless and spare,
  May their instructions be
The means to make our souls prepare
  For immortality.

Help us to love them as we ought,
  And worship only Thee,—
Thy just commands ne'er set at nought,
  And from temptations flee.

Our sins and errors we confess,
  O Lord, do Thou forgive;
Through Jesus Christ, our righteousness,
  Who died that we might live.

For all Thy goodness in the past,
  Accept our song of praise;
And grant we all may meet at last,
  A nobler strain to raise.

VERSES TO A YOUNG LADY ON LEAVING
SCOTLAND FOR ENGLAND.

SPRING'S early flowers will soon be here.
　To deck ilk bank and brae, Mary,
But ilka flower will kep a tear,
　Since thou art far away, Mary.

And whae will now their beauties trace,
　Wi' sic an art as thine, Mary,
And bend o'er theirs sae sweet a face?
　For yours was half divine, Mary.

By Lintie burn, the trysting tree
　Will flourish soon again, Mary;
But at the gloamin' hour we'll see
　Ane wander there alane, Mary.

And when the stars peep through the blue,
　And a' the wuds are still, Mary,
His heart will fondly turn to you,
　There wander where he will, Mary.

Auld Scotland mourns a flower away
　More sweet than England's rose, Mary,
But all thy charms my tuneless lay
　Can never half disclose, Mary.

I'll hang my harp by Gala's stream,
    Where nane shall hear its strain, Mary,
And your return will be the theme,
    If ever tuned again, Mary.

SONNET.

Howl, ye bleak winds, such music suits mine ear,
As here I pensive wander by the stream,
By Leithen's stream, where one in life's young
    dream,
So late our joy and solace left us here
To mourn, alas! and shed the bitter tear;
For never more to us he can return,
Since cruel death has now for ever torn
Him from us, whom we loved with love sincere;
His gentle looks methinks we still can see,
His music voice we think we still can hear;
But no! for now hath pass'd the fix'd decree
That took him even before the dying year;
We'll follow soon, another year begun
Bids us prepare, we ne'er may see it run.

IN MEMORY OF JANET HARDIE.

Who Died at Innerleithen, 27th December, 1876.
Aged 20 Years.

DEAR one! though gone, methinks I see
   The gentle looks thy sweet face bore,
But now hath pass'd the fix'd decree
   That took thee from us evermore.

For evermore, from this sad scene
   Of low deceit, and grief and pain,
Which thou hast seen, and felt, I ween,
   The brief time here thou didst remain.

Thy loving heart is now at rest,
   That heav'd in youth's affection strong,
And they who loved and knew thee best,
   Will cherish here thy memory long.

Though of perfection none may boast,
   But mourn o'er follies day by day,
Yet few hadst thou compared with most,
   Whom oft temptations lead astray.

Thy lovely face seem'd shaded o'er,
   As if some passive thoughts were thine,
And thy young heart felt to the core
   Some dark foreboding round it twine.

Sudden at last fell death's rude hand,
  That laid thee low as some fair flower,
When the fierce blast sweeps o'er the land,
  And wastes its beauty in an hour.

But now 'tis past, life's sickly dream
  Is over now, and all its woes;
We trust, thou'rt safe beside the stream
  Of pure delights and sweet repose.

And here we're left to mourn thy loss,
  And all the joy thy presence gave;
Here on the sea of life to toss,
  The sport of every surging wave.

But there's a haven to which thou'rt gone,
  We hope at last to meet, and be
Where separations there are none,
  In bliss throughout eternity.

TO THE NEW WOODEN BRIDGE OVER THE GALA.

HECH ! but ye're on yer legs at last,
To face the winter's stormy blast,
Where mony a roarin' flood rows past,
  Wi' thunderin' din ;
I hope ye're made baith firm and fast
  Wi' mony a pin.

To look across yer weel-raised back,
It seems as it would never rack,
And tho' ye may whiles craze and crack,
  Ye winna bend ;
I ken sae by yer vera mak'
  My timmer friend.

It's true yer heart's no made o' stane,
And ye'll gie mony a weary grane,
As did the auld ane, dead and gane,
  Wi' tear and wear,
But ye'll stand there, if left alane,
  For mony a year.

It's easy seen, on close inspection,
That ye're a braw and firm erection—

Thanks be to ane wha gied direction
　　How they should make ye,
And at the threaten'd interdiction
　　Did ne'er forsake ye.

Now streekit owre frae bank to bank,
And close o'erlaid wi' mony a plank,—
Haith! but his haffets I could clank,
　　Wha'd pu' ye down;
Whate'er his title, birth, or rank,
　　I'd break his crown.

But I'll no need to be sae rude,
For now I hope you don't intrude;
Folk see that ye're a public good
　　They couldna want;
Round by the stane ane ilka flood
　　Wad be a jaunt.

Now safe as on a turnpike road,
Baith auld and young can owre thee plod,
Even they wha hae an extra load
　　Can safely toddle,
When staggering hame to their abode
　　Light i' the noddle.

To keep the wind and water out,
They'll hae ye paintit sune, nae doubt,

And on yer buirdly shanks sae stout
    Ye'll brave the weather;
The water-wrack ye'll turn about
    Light as a feather.

For mony a year may ye be spared,
Wi' Tammas, yer auld freend and laird,
And near ye in his green kail-yard
    Lang may he dibble,
While leeks and tatties spring and braird
    To houk and nibble.

Now deckit out sae trig and braw,
Ye'll be a brig to mense us a',
And Galaleans, great and sma',
    Will sing thy praise,
Till frail and worn wi' age ye fa',
    To end yer days.

WRITTEN ON THE CENTENARY OF
SIR WALTER SCOTT.

AN hundred years have pass'd away,
Again returns the eventful day,
When kind auld Nature seem'd to say—
    Scotland, dear spot,
I bring, form'd from no common clay,
    The immortal Scott!

And to her charge she gave the boy,
Who lived to be our country's joy;
And here we're met, without annoy,
    To speak the praise
Of one whose works will never cloy,
    Till end of days.

Yes, Caledonia, stern and wild,
Received her darling, gifted child,
And nursed him up in manners mild,
    And art sublime;
The "Great Magician" now he's styled,
    Through every clime.

Lo, at his touch, what forms appear,
That mov'd in many a by-gone year,
And scenes that to us all endear,
        Our native land,
Pencil'd in outline, bold and clear,
        With master hand.

See Dandie Dinmont manly stride,
Wi' Harry Bertram at his side;
And Dominie Sampson, gaspin' wide,
        Shouting "Prodigious,"
At each event, which might betide
        Civil or religious.

And far up in yon highland glen,
See bold Rob Roy and a' his men,
Where Nicol Jarvie, too, we ken
        Was there seen danglin',
And red het poker'd, nine or ten,
        For wi' him wranglin'.

Major Galbraith, ye got yer fairin',
And fand the Bailie wasna' sparein',
When he sent through yer tartans flarin'
        The red-het poker,
Nae doubt ye thought he was a daurin',
        Queer auld joker.

It served ye right, ye damn'd the brandy
He offer'd on the spot to stand ye
To end the quarrel, and to bandy
    Nae mair high words;
But Jarvie's weapon proved as handy
    As Highland swords.

And auld Mause Headrigg, see her ride
High mounted, like a warlock's bride,
Her shrill voice raised, in wrath to chide,
    Yon bluidy crew,
That ranged the country far and wide
    For those they slew.

And Cuddy Headrigg, Mause's son,
Who, when the preachin' had begun,
Declared his mother far outrun,
    And bore the gree,
Owre Kettledrummle, yon great gun,
    'Gainst Papacy.

And Dousterswivel we survey,
The game he did Sir Arthur play;
And auld Monkbarn's eccentric way
    And queer nick-nackets,
How at St Ruth's he gied them pay,
    And het their jackets.

Auld Caleb Balderston behold,
Whom stern necessity made bold,
For honour o' the house we're told,
  Could lee or steal
The Cooper's dinner, hot or cold,
  Answer'd him weel.

But when the thunner storm came on,
The house's honour seem'd near gone ;
'Twas then puir Caleb gied a groan,
  And swore the thunner
Came doon the lum, wi' soot and stone,
  And spoilt the dinner.

Losh how he gar'd auld Mysie skirl,
Till a' thing in the house played dirl,
And then he made the dishes hurl,
  Wi' sic a dash,
That a' the inmates thought the warl'
  Had gane to crash.

Brave knights and ladies we survey,
The wise, the witty, grave, and gay ;
And warriors in the bloody fray
  And deadly strife
Stand yet before us, clear as day,
  Drawn to the life.

'Twere vain here to enumerate all,
And now we let the curtain fall,
And leave him in his magic hall,
　　　　While ne'er forgot,
Shall be the birthdays that recall
　　　　The name of Scott.

THE COTTER'S SONG.

My sang will be our ain fireside;
  There's nane sae sweet to me,
Wi' bairns to form a circle wide,
  And join wi' merry glee.

Sing merrily a', sing merrily a'
  A happy band are we;
Let haughty lords enjoy their ha',
  Our ain fireside for me.

The surly winds may blaw their warst,
  Our fire blinks bonnilie,
We've meal i' the house will ser' till hairst,
  Ill aff we canna be.
    Sing merrily a', &c.

Our crummie fills the milking pail,
  We've butter and we've cheese,
And grund aneuch to grow our kail,
  And plant our beans and pease—
    Sing merrily a', &c.

My thrifty wife, when claes wear out,
   Wi' needle and wi' shears,
On ilka hole can stitch a clout,
   And make them last for years.
       Sing merrily a', &c.

Thro' summer heat and winter's cauld,
   Content to work I'll be,
And when at last I'm worn and auld,
   The bairns they'll work for me.
       Sing merrily a', &c.

Thus happy in my low estate,
   I'll spend ilk passing year ;
So care and envy take the gate,
   Ye'll find nae shelter here.

   Sing merrily a', sing merrily a',
     A happy band are we ;
   Let haughty lords enjoy their ha',
     Our ain fireside for me.

IN MEMORY OF THE LATE
HUGH BORTHWICK, Shepherd, who Died at
Old Caberstone, 31st May, 1876, aged 53 years.

Mr Borthwick who, though he followed the humble and obscure occupation of a shepherd, was gifted with superior talents, and acquirements, was an excellent scholar, and wrote a good deal on scientific and useful subjects. He was the successful competitor for several prize essays, and which appeared in some of the Agricultural Magazines. The following verses were written in autumn, near Caberstone, where the writer had often the pleasure of seeing and conversing with him .—

THE autumn leaves are falling fast,
　From the old trees that skirt the way,
And howling through them, sweeps the blast,
　Foretelling soon cold winter's sway.

'Twas sweet, at close of summer's day,
　To wander here with those we loved ;
But one, alas ! hath pass'd away,
　In manhood's prime, by death removed.

And though, in shepherd's humble guise,
　He moved among us here obscure,
His cultur'd soul could soar, and rise,
　With those whose names shall long endure.

Ah, Borthwick ! thou hast left the scene,
   And here to us will ne'er return ;
But, memory keeps the laurels green,
   Which thou so gracefully hast worn.

When some fair tree uprooted lies,
   With fruit and foliage to the ground ;
We pause, and view it with surprise,
   And ponder on the ruin round.

Even so, when thou wast call'd away
   So suddenly, and from us torn,
We felt, and saw it with dismay,
   And love's affection bade us mourn.

Thy friends to Heaven's will resigned,
   Now see thy flock another's care ;
And hope, at last, to meet and find
   Thee in a world than this more fair.

And now, farewell, we trust thou'rt led
   By the Good Sheperd's gentle hand
Among his flock, in beauty clad,
   Immortal in the sinless land.

ADDRESS TO THE GALA VOLUNTEER.

By JOHN SHIELS, Author of Poetical Works.

Inserted here with permission.

["The subject which gave rise to the following poem was a letter which was published in the "Border Advertiser," signed "A Gala Volunteer," calling on the "braw lads," to volunteer and form themselves into a rifle corps, five hundred strong, to meet emergency in case of French invasion," &c.]

MY noble friend, I am sincere,
A lover of my country dear;
I am a sterling volunteer,
        At your command,
To fecht the French wi' gun or spear,
        On sea or land;

Providin' that ye dinna slicht
Me, just because I'm scarcely heicht,
And little mair than jockey weicht,
        Or I wad e'en
A gallant soldier, wrang or richt,
        To serve the Queen.

But, man, I think there's little fear
O' French invaders comin' here,
But if they do, I vow and swear
  To rin wi' speed,
And help to make their passage dear
  Wi' poother and lead.

The British Lion, trusty chap,
His teeth are still as sharp to snap,
As when he foucht wi' Uncle Nap,
  O' great renown,
And tore frae his immortal scalp
  The braw French crown.

Although his rigid nephew, Lew',
Has vow'd revenge for Waterloo,
Our land to conquer and subdue,
  Believe my word,
His hands are tichtly tied the noo
  Wi' Austrian cord.

If Tear'm really is yer name,
I'd like the number o' yer hame,
And if ye let me hae the same,
  And treat me cooth,
I'll ca', and crack aboot the scheme
  By word o' mooth.

Our braw lads hae nae time for drill,
At least I hae nae time mysel',
We are sae busy at Tweed Mill .
    Maist ilka nicht
Our faulders thump away pell-mell
    To half-past eight.

But if ye take me as I am,
To fecht the French whene'er they come,
I'll make the rifle bullets bum
    Wi' nature's skill,
And rough and ready rule o' thumb,
    The French to kill.

O' enemies ye hae a pair
At hame, that bit ye rather sair,
But if they fash ye ony mair,
    As sure as death,
War openly I will declare
    Against them baith.

And if your bold sarcastic foes
In open field do me oppose,
For this my note in rhyme and prose,
    Their spite to vend,
Then for the gauntlet on it goes,
    For right defend.

Yon sour-plum-toddy sodger loon,
Wha's heart lies surely in his shoon,
To treat ye in a style like you,
    Sae indiscreet,
I hae the mind to knock him doon
    When next we meet.

He says he longs to see you strut
In Merry Andrew's kind o' suit,
O' plush kneebreeks and crimson coat,
    In martial glory,
And crowns ye wi' a cockit hat,
    To grace his story.

Noo just make ye the grand attack,
And I'm the chiel stands at your back;
And if their croons we dinna crack,
    We'll let them see,
It shanna be for want o' pluck
    By you and me.

REPLY TO MR J. SHIELS.

" Does haughty Gaul invasion threat?
  Then let the loons beware, sir;
There's wooden wa'ls upon our seas,
    And volunteers on shore, sir."—BURNS.

MAN, Johnnie, but ye're gallant mettle ;
Wi' men like you we sune wad settle
The French, or ony foreign cattle
      In shape o' foe,
As easy as I'd crush a nettle
      Just at a'e blow.

Ye're no like yon twa coward chiels,
Whase hearts beat down aboot their heels :
But just a man whom Galashiels
        May weel be proud o'—
It's men like you our nation feels
        We stand in need o'.

Altho' ye're maybe nae great heicht
And little mair than jockey weicht,
The deil a fear but ye could fecht,
      If ance in wrath ;
Think how wee Davie served yon knicht,
        Goliah o' Gath.

Wi' sic as you just at my back,
How their French jackets I wad thwack!
If e'er they make the bold attack,
　　They'll get their licks,
Their spindle-shanks and heads we'll hack
　　Like green fir sticks.

Our prisoners, John, will clear the vermin
About our fields and gardens swarmin';
To hear them gibber French, how charmin'!
　　And see them eat
Live paddies, croakin' most alarmin',
　　Will be a treat.

It's surely time that we get arm'd,
When folk are gettin' sae alarm'd,
And hae our bluid and spirits warm'd,
　　To take the field;
Thick they may come as bees new swarm'd,
　　Wi' sword and shield.

Come owre some night or it be lang,
As sune as ye get through yer thrang,
And to the magistrate we'll gang—
　　Hear his opinion,
How we could raise an army strang
　　For his dominion.

Ye'll hear folk talk about expense,
Losh, man, they hae but little sense,
To think that for the sake o' pence
    They'll risk invasion ;
Awa wi' ony sic pretence
    At this occasion.

O wad some power assist my rhyme,
And gar the verses rightly chime,
I'd make them sound through a' our clime,
    Baith far and near,
Till thousands rush, and lose nae time,
    To volunteer.

Auld Scotia, wi' thy towering hills,
Thy gushing burns and gurgling rills,
Wi' love to thee my heart aye fills—
    Our native land,
Thee, while life's blood my bosom thrills,
    I will defend.

Long life to our illustrious Queen,
Whose like is scarcely ever seen ;
Her gracefu' form and modest mien
    We a' adore ;
Around her throne may laurels green
    Twine evermore.

THE DEATH O' JOHNNIE'S HOOLET.

STERN death, that grim, relentless carle,
A'e night into an auld beer barrel
Sent Johnnie's hoolet wi' a hurl
   Clean heels owre head,
And left it there to end the quarrel,
   Cauld, stiff, and dead.

'Twas but a hoolet, some will say,
Sae let it gang, it's weel away;
But Johnnie's heart next morn was wae,
   And little wonder—
Its like ye wadna seen nae day
   Among a hunder.

Like daws it didna reive and steal;
And then it likeit him sae weel,
And follow'd close just at his heel
   When he cried " Jock ! "
After himsel' he ca'd the chiel—
   For 'twas a cock !

By Tailor W——n it was catch'd
Near Langshaw tower, where it was hatch'd,

Syne frae the Fairy Dean was fetch'd
    To Galashiels—
A town for braw lads yet unmatch'd
    And spinnin' wheels.

For days 'twas shifted up and doon
Among the urchins o' the toon ;
Its life nae doubt wad very soon
    Been at an end,
But Johnnie saved it frae ilk loon,
    And stood its friend.

He learn'd it sune to be sae wise,
Losh, had ye seen't among the mice.
It sneckit them like in a vice,
    Then raised its claw,
And swallow'd them just in a trice,
    Skin, banes, and a'.

It had a curious face, I ween,
Wi' its queer neb, but then its e'en
Were full and black—their like's ne'er seen ;
    I ne'er saw ony :
They might hae graced out mony a queen
    Some folk ca' bonnie.

It ne'er was tether'd in a string,
But free to soar upon the wing ;

THE DEATH O' JOHNNIE'S HOOLET.

Yet ne'er like other birds in spring
  Wad flee away,
But lived as happy as a king
  Frae day to day.

For mony a year it lived wi' Johnnie—
Was visited by mony a cronie,
To see its e'en, sae dark and bonnie,
  Forbye to trace
Its physiognomy sae funny,
  And queer round face.

But never, 'neath the moon's pale light,
We'll hear its scream at silent night;
The vital spark has ta'en its flight,
  Ne'er to return,
While Johnnie's left a wofu' wight,
  Its loss to mourn.

VERSES.

Recited on Old Year's Night after Supper, when the fare was a Scotch Haggis.

YEAR after year is gliding past,
Wearin' the wheels o' life doun fast ;
But joy be wi' us while they last,
      And now and then a haggis.

I've been at mony a merry spree,
Wi' jovial cronies, kind and free !
But ne'er had sic a nicht o' glee,
      As lately owre a haggis.

That happy nicht I'll ne'er forget,
When owre at Johnnie Shiel's we met,
A' round a table neatly set,
      Crown'd wi' a reekin' haggis.

When Johnnie he pu'd out the pin,
And wi' a grace, said, "now begin,"
Sune down ilk face the sweat did rin,
      Wi' plyin' at the haggis.

It wasna eaten just in crumbs,
Our gutty wames were bent like drums,
The vera chairs aneath our b——s
     Crazed wi' their load o' haggis.

"Syne Johnnie wi' the whisky cam',
And gied us a' a thumpin' dram,"
To qualify the enormous cram
     We'd eaten o' the haggis.

Wi' sangs and recitations round,
The roof and rafters did resound;
Wi' social joy that night was crown'd,
     When met at Johnnie's haggis.

Just sic a nicht may we hae here,
Till morning brings a guid new year;
And may we ever hae sic cheer,
     As just a good Scotch haggis.

May fortune kindly bless ye a',
Wi' guid braid claith to make ye braw,
And shield ye frae the frost and snaw,
     Wi' health to eat a haggis.

SONG.

Respectfully inscribed to Mr JAMES ROBERTSON, first Presi-
dent of the Burns' Club, Galashiels.   Written for, and sung
at, their meeting for the Celebration of the Poet's Birthday.

Tune—" SAIR, SAIR, WAS MY HEART, &c."

Now, to boast the name of one
    Whom we can ne'er forget,
Again, in love and harmony,
    A social band we're met.
Our toast will be the memory
    Of Burns, the Bard so rare,
Who tuned his harp sae sweetly
    On the banks o' the Ayr.

Ah! nevermair he'll wander
    Beside the classic stream,
That soothed him wi' its murmurs,
    When in life's troubled dream
He sadly mused and ponder'd,
    Oppress'd wi' grief and care,
And sang the dirge sae mournfu',
    On the banks o' the Ayr.

Yet happy hours flew o'er him,
  Though swift they were and few,
When wanderin' wi' the lassie
  He loved so leal and true;
And vow'd wi' warm devotion
  The vows he'll pledge nae mair,
To his dear Highland Mary,
  On the banks o' the Ayr.

Auld Scotland weel may boast him,
  Nor view him wi' disdain;
She nevermair among her sons
  May see his like again.
And O! he lo'ed her dearly,
  As weel his sangs declare,
And proudly were they chanted
  On the banks o' the Ayr.

Though now his voice is silent,
  His sangs are wi' us still;
To-night upon the passing breeze
  We'll waft them wi' guid will,
And cherish still his mem'ry;
  ·For wha can e'er compare
Wi' him that sang sae sweetly
  On the banks o' the Ayr?

A HYMN.

In darkness let thy face shine bright,
　　Lead us, O Lord, to follow Thee—
To walk as children of the light,
　　And then how sweet our path will be.

Along the safe and narrow way
　　Fain would we journey; be our guide,
And where temptations lead astray,
　　Do Thou, O Lord, be at our side.

Too long, alas! we've wander'd far
　　From Thee, along destruction's road,
Thou Star of Bethlehem, be our star!
　　God of our fathers, be our God!

Turn Thou our feet from paths of sin,
　　And fill our hearts with warmer love
For Him that died, that we might win
　　Eternal life with Him above.

As strangers in a foreign land,
　　We have no habitation here;
As Thou hast led Thy chosen band,
　　So lead us through this desert drear.

Strengthen our faith, that we may view
The far-off land, so passing fair;
And hope will cheer us to pursue
The promised joys for ever there.

Such is the guidance, Lord, we need
In all our wanderings here below;
For Jesus' sake, we humbly plead
That Thou such favour wouldst bestow.

And when life's pilgrimage is o'er,
May we at last, though toss'd and driven
Across the Jordan reach the shore,
To pour our grateful hearts in Heaven.

SONNET.

On wings of Faith how sweet to soar away,
  To boundless realms of everlasting bliss;
  The fetter'd soul pants in a world like this
For purer joys, nor here would wish to stay.
As strangers here, alas! we do but stray
  Far from our home in this drear wilderness—
  From those we loved, now gone, and sadly miss,
But mourn not, for, I ween, far happier they.
And why are we left lagging here behind,
  Ye ransom'd ones, that form that happy band?
Is it that we're impure in heart and mind,
  Therefore unfit for that fair sinless land?
Then O! my soul, prize well the time now given;
Even here below we must begin our heaven.

TO THE SABBATH.

WELCOME thy hours of peace and rest,
    Sweet type of Heaven;
'Mong other days, thou art the best
    Of all the seven.
Oft as we rise to greet thy morn,
    Our prayer shall be,
While earth remains, may the toil-worn
    Find rest in thee!

When first creation smiling stood
    Beneath yon sun,
With all that moved in field and flood,
    And work was done;
Well-pleased their Maker then view'd o'er
    His finish'd plan,
And bless'd the day, for evermore
    A boon to man.

And who shall dare the pledge profane
    Of love divine?
For low pursuits or worldly gain
    Mar its design?

Thou blessed day of calm delight
    And sweet repose,
May all thy hours be spent aright
    Till ages close.

How fair yon sun, when breaks thy morn
    Through shades of night,
That smiles o'er all with beams unshorn
    In splendour bright!
But fairer He who from the tomb
    Triumphant rose,
Dispelling fear, and doubt, and gloom,
    And all our foes

Day when Christian pilgrims meet—
    A weary band—
And speak of promised rest complete
    In Canaan's land.
On wings of faith they soar away
    From earth's dull scene,
To brighter worlds of endless day
    And joy serene.

With souls refresh'd they start anew
    Their Christian race,
And long for Heaven's bright land in view,
    With quickening pace.

When all their weary wanderings cease,
 And toils are o'er,
There they shall dwell in joy and peace
 For evermore.

While o'er life's rough and thorny road
 We burden'd stray,
We still shall rest our weary load
 In thee, blest day.
Welcome thy hours of peace and rest,
 Sweet type of Heaven ;
'Mong other days, thou are the best
 Of all the seven!

MUSINGS.

LATE at summer's eve I stray'd
Through this smiling woodland scene,
Where I met my ain true love,
Tripping o'er the verdant green.
Beauty glow'd upon her cheek,
Love was in her soft blue een.
At our feet the flowers were springing;
O'er our heads the wee birds sang;
And in softest, sweetest measures,
Through the woods their echoes rang.
Hand in hand, with hearts o'erflowing,
Here in joy we stray'd alang.

In yon sweet secluded spot,
Where no prying eye might see,
There I pressed her to my heart,
'Neath the flow'ring hawthorn tree,
Many a pledge of love, I ween,
There, my lost one gave to me.
Rosy blush'd the sun, then setting;
Soft the evening shadows fell;
Scented birks perfumed the breezes,
Sighing through the forest dell;
And like sad, departing voices,
Breathing softly fare-thee-well.

There we told the tales of love,
" Pledging oft to meet again ;"
Ah! how short-lived were the joys,
And our hopes, alas! how vain :
As a dream, from which we wake
To a world of grief and pain.
Darker lour'd the shades of evening
O'er the landscape, dim and grey ;
Soon the very heavens seem'd scowling ;
Birds sat mute on every spray ;
Through the trees, the moaning breezes
Seem'd to mourn the parting day.

Sounds that night fell on mine ear—
Whispers strange, words ne'er can tell,
And that meeting was our last
'Neath the hawthorn in the dell ;
Where to me the breezes sigh
Dismal yet, as passing bell.
Now 'tis winter ; sad I wander
Where so often we have met,
Or near by yonder lone churchyard,
Where the sun seems ever set,
O'er the grave where now she slumbers,
Whom I loved, nor can forget.

S O N G.

WHEN first I saw thy bonnie face,
   And sweet glance o' thine e'e, lassie,
You seem'd as ane sent to replace
   The joys long fled frae me, lassie.

Long had I stray'd by yonder burn,
   For weary hours alane, lassie,
And mused on joys that ne'er return
   To cheer the heart again, lassie.

Thy smile was as the morning light,
   That ushers in the day, lassie,
And sheds o'er all a radiance bright,
   On every bank and brae, lassie.

And ever since the hour we met,
   Hast thou been true to me, lassie ;
Believe me then, I'll ne'er forget
   To love and live for thee, lassie.

BUY THE TRUTH, AND SELL IT NOT."

PROVERBS.

THE trifles we on earth pursue
When grasp'd, we strive for something new ;
Unsatisfied, our hearts still pant
For something yet our natures want.
The wise man felt the void within,
And knew the false delights of sin ;
O may his words ne'er be forgot—
" Buy the truth, and sell it not."

And what is truth ?   Let Scripture tell ;
Christ came from heaven to save from hell :
He is the Way, the Truth, the Life,
And peace He gives where all was strife—
Peace which the world can never give,
Nor take from those who in Him live.
His word is truth, yes, every jot—
" Buy the truth, and sell it not."

The poorest here this truth can buy ;
'Tis freely offer'd, wherefore die ?
One has already paid the sum—
" Ho ! every one that thirsteth come ; "

And he that hath no money shall
Drink freely from Salvation's well.
Then come, though humble be your lot—
"Buy the truth, and sell it not."

O sell it not for aught below,
Where all is but a fleeting show;
Here riches oft take wings and fly,
And pleasures sicken, droop and die;
Each earthly hope at last will seem
A phantom, or an idle dream.
These words ne'er from the mem'ry blot—
"Buy the truth, and sell it not."

When comes the great and solemn day,
When heaven and earth shall pass away,
May we amongst the number be
Of those at last whom truth sets free.
Aught else will then seem false and vain,
And yield us nought but grief and pain.
That we be found then without spot,
"Buy the truth, and sell it not."

AN EPISTLE.

BY THE LATE MR WILLIAM LAMB,
PROFESSOR OF MUSIC.

Inserted here with the kind permission of his near relatives, we believe it will be read and appreciated by many of his old pupils who survive him ; and the public in general, for he was beloved and highly respected by all who knew him Though bereft of eyesight from early youth, his proficiency as a teacher and composer of music was astonishing.

On sending Mr Lamb a copy of the first edition of this book, with the lines :—

> " And though thine eyes, alas ' are dim.
> To thee, some friend will read my lays,
> And bid thee sometimes think of him
> Whose lyre you tuned in other days."

The following was sent in reply :—

" DEAR SIR, The book, the pledge ye sent,
    O' friendship an' regard,
  A welcome present is to me,
    Frae sic an honoured bard.

" Altho' I ne'er could mak' twa lines
    O' simple crambo clink ;
  I'm fairly forced to try my hand,
    A word or twa to link.

" An' first I maun express my thanks,
    For sic a pleasing gift ;
  Losh man, the very mention o't,
    Gies my auld heart a lift.

" A book—a book o' poetry—
　　The author, friend o' mine ;
　O may there muckle guid come o'
　　His dealings wi' the NINE.

" Surrounded as I am, south here,
　　Wi' ships, an' coal, an' smoke ;
　The " Pockpuddin's " themselves, wi' brains
　　No unlike sandstane rock.

" How fresh an' sweet your lyre does sound
　　Frae bonnie Gala side ;
　It brings to mind far happier days
　　Than e'er can now betide.

" It brings to mind thae happy days—
　　Thae days o' auld langsyne—
　Whase memories like " ivy green "
　　Around my auld heart twine.

" Ye'll mind thae days as weel's as mysel',
　　An' things that happened then ;
　When Jamie Mather an' the rest
　　Wi' us were but and ben.

" When George, the Elder, honest man
　　Cam' courtin' Maggie Scott ;
　An' Gilbert tae was trying hard,
　　To pick ane oot the lot.

" O' lassies young an' fair that cam';
    To schule to learn to sing;
But often learnt to tie themselves
    Wi' vows an' wedding ring.

" Ye'll mind fu' weel o' Mather's shop,
    Where sangs an' glees we tried;
Where mony a laugh an' joke we had,
    An' very seldom sighed.

" These a' hae gane, thae scenes, and friends.
    Are widely scattered noo;
The grass grows green whar' some are laid
    Whase hearts were leal an' true.

" The time comes on wi' hasty flicht,
    For me to follow tae,
But may ye lang be spared, my friend
    To tune your pleasant lay.

" An' may ye sing o' truth an' worth,
    Do a' the guid ye can;
An' maybe ye may help to mak',
    Man brother be to man.

" An' noo this letter I maun close
    An' thankfu', sure, I am
That I can sign mysel' your friend
    Yours truly, WILLIAM LAMB.

EXCURSION TO THE LOCHS.

St Mary's, Loch Skene, and the Grey Mare's Tail.

Many years have elapsed since I first visited the far-famed lochs in the land of Hogg, Tibbie Shiel, and Jenny O' Birkhill. As it may be interesting to relate what I saw and heard in my few days excursion, and give anecdotes in connection with the ladies named, I will do so in my own simple way, hoping to give pleasure to some, and offence to none.

It was a bright July morning, when free from toil, I sauntered with a friend by the side of a little wooded park on the banks of the Tweed, where a handsome, dappled grey mare was idly grazing. Thought I, if you were mine, how soon would I be astride your back, and away in "Tam O' Shanter" style to see Tibbie Shiel, our modern "Lady of the Lake," and quoting the lines from Burns.

> " I've sturdy legs, the Lord be thankit !
>   And a' my gates on foot I'll shankit."

The matter was settled at once, my esteemed friend agreeing to accompany me to the land of the wondrous shepherd bard, for—

Ne'er was shepherd lad sae giftit;
  Whae could sing sae sweet a strain ?
And his harp, say, whae can lift it,
  Tune its silent strings again ?

We wandered on along the banks of the Tweed till we crossed the bridge by way of Traquair, passed the grey, old mansion with its surroundings, and which, evidently, Sir Walter Scott had in his eye when he wrote his first fine novel, " Waverley," and introduced there the young hero of the work, to the " Baron Bradwardine " Passing next through the quiet little village of Traquair, to the right, on the hill-top, is seen the clump of trees called the "Bush abune Traquair," which has been made famous in song. Proceeding onwards through beautiful scenery, we soon came to the steep hill-road, called "Paddy's Slack" with nothing to speak of, but, that we went sweating, and feverish under a burning sun, for miles away on the moorlands without meeting a human being, till at last we came to a cadger, who seemed to be an old bachelor, in converse with a blooming young damsel, and making her laugh most joyously. Probably the talk would

be of love, mixed with fresh butter, eggs and
chickens. Wearied and thirsty, we asked the
cadger how far it was to the Gordon Arms Inn ?
Pointing to a far off turn in the road, he said,
'Div ye see yon turn?" We said "Yes." "Weel,
as sune as ye're roond yon turn, ye'll find the
smell o' the toddy."   Leaving the pair, we went
on till we passed the turn pointed out, and came
to Mount Benger, where the shepherds around
were gathered, and busily engaged in sheep-
shearing, this being called, clipping time.   We
were now in the land of Hogg, and where, an-
nually in times gone by, he would meet with his
neighbours here for the same work, while his
poetic fancy was soaring away to other objects
than the dumb animals bound before them
undergoing the shearing process.   And here, we
thought, he might have composed that exquisite
and most musical of his compositions, his " Ode
to the Skylark," beginning with—

> " Bird of the wilderness,
>   Blithsome and cumberless ;
> Sweet be thy matin o'er moorland and lea,
>   Emblem of happiness,
>   Blest is thy dwelling place ;
> O, to abide in the desert with thee ! "

And farther on in the piece—we cannot omit

one favourite verse, as describing the upward
flight of the charming songster in its full gush
of melody.

> " O'er fell and fountain sheen,
>   O'er moor and meadow green,
> O'er the red streamers that herald the day,
>   Over the cloudlet dim,
>   Over the rainbows rim ;
> Musical cherub ! Hie, hie thee away ! "

But, as neither men nor birds can live on
poetry and song alone, we made for the com-
modious Inn, called the "Gordon Arms," which
we soon reached, and drank to the memory of
James Hogg, the Ettrick Shepherd.   Having
rested, and refreshed ourselves with the good
things of this excellent establishment, we resumed
our journey, and a few miles brought us to the
lower end of St Mary's Loch.   The outlet of this
loch forms the beginning of the Yarrow, which
has been consecrated to song and poetry, and
made dear to all hearts wherein dwells the love
of music, especially, of the sad, yet pleasing kind,
brought out by the many old ballads sung in
pensive strains, of sad events, and sorrowful
scenes which tradition recounts, all the way
down this romantic stream.   St Mary's Loch is a
beautiful sheet of water, three and a half miles

in length, a mile in breadth, and seven in circum-
ference, the average depth said to be 150 feet, or
30 feet deeper than the Baltic; soundings being
taken many years ago by a retired captain.   We
had now, a pleasant walk before us, a gentle
breeze stirred the surface of the lake, making its
little wavelets in quick succession kiss the shores
that cradle its beauteous waters.   And gazing
across to the south side, a fine scene meets the
eye, pasture land of the richest green, with easy
slope, stretches far as the eye can reach, and
dotted over with nibbling fleecy flocks, which on
the

> " Bonnie banks all in a swarm do go."

When we reached the upper end of the loch,
the first object of interest we saw was the "Hogg
Monument," which stands a short distance from
the road side, to the right on a piece of rising
ground ; the base is a four square substantial
looking erection, ornamented at each corner with
a ram's head and horns, the statue seated with
crook, and plaid, and the dog at the feet, the
whole looks very natural.   On the base, we read
the lines engraved, and which are we suppose
quoted from his own writings ; they are we
think, most appropriate, and truly characteristic
of the man :—

At silent eve in lonely dale,
He kept strange converse with the gale—
Held worldly pomp in high derision ,
And wander'd in a world of vision.

The monument is the design and workmanship
of Mr Currie, Darnick, near Melrose, and reflects
much to his fine taste and genious.   The sun
was now sinking behind the hills, and we took
the road across the small strip of land that
divides the lochs—St Mary's and the Loch of the
Lowes, where in a quiet corner between them
stands the cottage of Tibbie Shiel.   We knocked
at the door, and a decent looking old lady came
out, whom, we asked, if this was Tibbie Shiel's ?
" Aye," she said, " This is just Tibbie Shiels."
When I made apology for using the plain fami-
liar name " Oh," she said, " I never get any other
name than Tibbie, an I dinna want ony other
name than Tibbie, an' I believe this place 'ill be
ca'd Tibbie Shiel's lang after I'm deid, an' may be
to the end o' the world ; " and taking our hand,
bade us welcome, where we made arrangement
to make it our home for the night, and received
every attention and kindness, and we marvel not
that the late Henry Sanderson, of Galashiels,
complimented her so highly when he wrote the
poem commencing :—

"What's Yarrow but a river bare"?
Said Wordsworth, that puir peevish chiel;
I trow he'd found nae bareness there,
Had he but kent kind Tibbie Shiel."

After having refreshments of the best sort,
our good landlady brought to our room the
"Visitors' Books" saying they might amuse us,
and so they did. As the night wore on, my
companion suggested that "we go ben to the
kitchen fireside, and have a chat with Tibbie"
before going to rest, and we enjoyed her company
very much, as she recounted over the celebraties
that had visited the place. We told her that we
had put our names amongst them in the book,
with the addition of some remarks of a humorous
sort. And Tibbie said, "Weel, ye should not hae
dune that, an' I'll tell ye what for, ye dinna ken
what the next anes 'ill write ahint ye." And
then she went on to tell us, "how a grand pairty
ance cam to the hoose, an' amang them was a
countess, an' a lord, an' they wrote their names,
sayin' "they had newly arrived frae the continent."
"Weel, guess ye, what some ane o' the next visitors
had the impidence to dae? just to write, 'An'
whae the deevil cares whan ye cam frae the
Continent.'" We told her of a special night
which we had heard of, when a wedding party

was with her, and spent a jolly night, and amongst
them were Professor Wilson and Hogg. And in the
morning, after a short sleep, a number of them
were very thirsty, calling for water, water, ?
And Hogg, turning to her, called out,—" Tibbie ;
just gang away out; an bring in the Loch "
Tibby told us, " She minded fine o' that nicht,
but the Professor wasna there, but Hogg was
there, wi' his fiddle, an' played maist a' the nicht,
an' thae were his verra words." Having passed
a most enjoyable evening we retired to rest, and
rose early next morning to prepare for the rest
of our journey. On looking from our bedroom
window, we had a fine view right up the Loch of
the Lowes. It is smaller than St Mary's, and
only a mile in length, but thought to be of
greater depth. We turned again to the Moffat
road, and took our way for Birkhill. And now
the scene gradually changes from one of quiet
beauty to those of wilder aspect, all the way to
Loch Skene, which some one has described, and
truthfully,—" A scene of savage sublimity." As
we go along, and with the indulgence of those
who may read this, I will give some verses,
written on this excursion, at the request of Jenny
of Birkhill, and sent her a short time after, and
if any critics, who may peruse them, be so gentle

in their criticism as was Jenny, I shall not
regret my effort to please them.

Away, let's away, to the Grey Mare's Tail,
In a boat on Loch Skene, O sweetly we'll sail
Until the sun sets o'er the high saddle yoke;
Then, we'll fasten our boat secure to the rock,
We'll tie up our rod, having winded our reel,
And hoist on our shoulders a weel laden creel,
To hie down the mountain, where joys wait us
    still,
With the kind, hearty folks in the house at
    Birkhill.

Away, let's away, where the cliffs rise sublime,
And mock at the ravage of " Old Father Time,"
Where the wild water leaps from the far dizzy
    height,
And grumbles below like an angry sprite;
'Till spent 'mid the foam of the beautiful strife,
Serenely and calm, like a fair thing of life,
It wanders away at " its own sweet will,"
And laves the green banks by the foot o' Birkhill.

Away, let's away, where the long grass waves,
And the winds lonely sigh o'er the martyrs'
    graves;
'Twas there in the beauteous green temple of God,
The miscreant Claver'se impiously strode,

And pour'd out the blood of the great and the
    good
Who, true to the Covenant, so firmly had stood;
But their bodies were all the murderer could kill,
Their souls sprang to God, from the scene at
    Birkhill.

Away, let's away where no sound meets' the ear,
But those which the wise and the good love to
    hear—
The song of the laverock far up in the cloud,
Where ofttimes the eagle screams piercing and
    loud ;
The rush of the waterfall, and the wild hiss,
As it dashes below to the rocky abyss,
While, sparkling 'mid sunbeams, sings many a
    rill,
As they journey to meet by the foot o' Birkhill.

Away, let's away, it is good to be there,
And leave for a season each earth-born care,
To stray where the Minstrel of Ettrick has
    strayed,
And con o'er the strains his sweet harp has
    played—
To watch the blue loch as unruffled it lies,
While mirror'd beneath sleeps the fair earth and
    skies ;

And drink from the fountain of pleasure our fill
At the banquet Dame Nature spreads out at
    Birkhill.

Having travelled a few miles on this lonely
road, we met a mysterious looking little man,
with a very swarthy complexion, with rings in
his ears, and a barrel organ on his back, we spoke,
but he only shook his head saying in a sort of
broken English—" Can't understand you."   And
here in what has been called fairy land—the
region where fancy holds sway, and forms by its
creative power, images and matter for fairy
literature.   Hogg, we thought, could have found
the mysterious looking stranger we met, a fit
subject for another " Brownie o' Bodsbeck."

That there have been elves and fairies,
    Hogg could whiles ha'e gien his aith,
When he wander'd by St Mary's,
    'Mid the scenes that nurse sic faith.

Oft he saw their moonlit capers
    If what a' is said be true,
Clad in green wi' mouse-skin slippers
    Sipping pearly draps o' dew.

As we went on, the scenery, in bold outline,
showed itself to be the "land of the mountain and
the flood," and from the headlands, numerous

streams of sparkling water came leaping and
tumbling down the ravines made in the steep hill
sides, right and left of us all the way. But the one
important object to be seen, and were getting
impatient to see, was the "Grey Mare's Tail,"
and in passing the numerous waterfalls, each one
we saw of larger volume than another, my
companion would point to, and say, "Will yon be
the Tail yet." Trudging onwards for miles, we at
last saw before us Birkhill, and which we may
say is in Barkshire, as about a dozen collie dogs
came rushing to meet us, all barking in chorus,
and wagging their tails in token of welcome.
Having entered the residence of Jenny and her
worthy consort, Mr Broadfoot, the shepherd, we
soon found ourselves "quite at home." A fine
hearty couple they were, who supplied our wants
with the best their house could afford, and gave
us direction to the "Gray Mare's Tail, and Loch
Skene, with a caution of the peril in our attempt-
ing to climb in a wrong course the precipitous
cliff. They told us a sad story of a son they had,
who lost his life by falling down the precipice,
in a snow storm   The hills here are so steep,
the shepherd told us, that when the sheep ailed
any way, and lay down, they did not lie two
minutes, but tumbled over to the bottom, and

when any were amissing, he sought for them
down the burn, and found them dead.   Having
been introduced, by my companion, as one of the
poetic tribe, I was requested to give them a
recitation of something original, and of my own
composition, which I did, and gave them a
humorous rhymed story, entitled "The Lucky
Night." I had not given many lines, when the
shepherd stopped me saying, 'just stop a minute
or two, till I bring in the folk." And wondering
where the folks were coming from, to our surprise,
the room was filled in a little, with young shep-
herds and others, with another addition of collies,
and, though no elocutionist, my effort to please
was crowned with success, amid the clapping of
hands, loud laughter, and the mingled chorus,
from the collie members of Barkshire.   I will
here relate an incident, to show that Jenny,
though a kind hearted lady, was one of high
spirit, in fact a heroine, who could hold her own
when occasion required her.   One day on going
round to the back of her dwelling, and leaving a
girl only in the kitchen, a tramp entered, and
was eyeing some fine hams hung from the ceiling;
so on Jenny coming in, he said—" You have some
good hams there, Missus." "O, aye," said Jenny.
" Well, I'll just help myself to one of them," said

the would-be thief. "I've just ae question to ask
ye, ma man," said Jenny.   "And what is it?" said
the tramp. "Did ony body see ye come in?"
"No, devil a one."   "Na," replied Jenny, "Nor,
the deevil a ane will ever see ye gang oot," and
turning to the girl sharply cried—"hand me that
axe, lassie," and the cowardly thief bolted from
the house. On another occasion, when Jenny,
along with a female friend, were crossing the
hills, on some needful errand, late one afternoon,
a thick mist settled down, and night coming on,
they lost their way, and resolved to sit down, or
lie on the hill till morning light came. Jenny's
companion, being of a pious disposition, sat con-
soling herself by singing hymns, and had started
the 23rd psalm as far as—

> "The Lord's my shepherd, I'll not want,"
> He makes me down to lie,"

And Jenny chimed in with—"Aye, haith, an
He's made us to lie doon in green pastures this
night, at ony rate."   When about to proceed on
our way, we were told to wait a little, as an
illustrious visitor was expected in a short time.
And soon a carriage drove up to the door, when
out stept a middle-aged lady of frank bearing,
and to our surprise, we had the pleasure of being
introduced to the Honourable Mrs Norton, so

well-known in literary circles. In our short
conversation about the weather and the scenery
around us, we learned that she was a frequent
visitor at this season, and enjoyed this quiet re-
treat very much. Taking our leave, and walking
a mile farther, from the Moffat road we now saw
the far-famed Gray Mare's Tail, so named from
the form it takes in its descent to the boiling
cauldron below. Turning to the right we went
by a footpath, and passed on our left, the graves
of the Cameronians who had met there in the
bygone days of persecution, and were slaughtered
by Claverhouse and his party. A dry stone dyke
encircles the spot.

When we came to the bottom of the fall, we
found the loose stones, mostly of an oval shape,
and finely smoothed by the continual turning,
caused by the falling water. Here the footpath
ended, as few attempt to go farther. Only one
side is accessible, that on the left, and we com-
menced the ascent of 300 feet near the edge of
the fall On looking upwards the sight was
magnificent, yet, appalling, the grass was scorch-
ed by a burning sun, and rendered so slippery,
that we durst not stir a foot until we had a
catch of the stunted grass in our hands all the
way. In this way we ascended, and once only,

looked back, when more than half way up, where
the sound, as if a thousand serpents were hissing,
as the waters fell on a projecting piece of rock,
sending the shivered mass around us, soft as dew,
in silken beauty, as they glistened in the sum-
mer's sun.   Arriving at the top of this, almost
perpendicular and gigantic cliff, we followed the
course of the stream till we came to its outlet
from Loch Skene.   The waters of this loch are
very dark, and lie sunk, as in a huge basin on
the top of the hill; and from this elevation on
looking across the lonely lake is seen the
high Saddle Yoke. It rises abruptly from the
water's edge, bare and stern, towering aloft
in sharp and distinct outline, as seen between us
and the azure sky to the height of 2400 feet at
an average with others in this wild and mountain-
ous district, and properly called, the highlands in
the south of Scotland. Not a tree, nor bush or
hedge could we see, in this wild region, nor the
chirp of a small bird could we hear, to break the
stillness that settled around. A feeling of extreme
loneliness steals over the mind, and we may quote
the lines from a poem by J. Truman, which will
express the effect.

   "The vision vast, the lone large sky,
     The kingly charm of mountains high,

The boundless silence, woke in me,
   Abstraction, reverence, reverie."

Leaving this scene of " Nature's wildest gran-
deur," and after plodding a long way through a
sort of peat moss, and leaping numerous gaps
filled with water, we made a safe descent to our
quarters again at Birkhill.   When we made our
departure, the worthy pair, Jenny and her hus-
band, escorted us a full mile on our way, where
we parted to see them no more, as they have now
gone the way of all the earth, and so has our
kind hostess, Tibbie Shiel.   For the comfort of
others, who may visit the charming scenery in
the land of Hogg, we may add, that the friends
left by Jenny and Tibby, and who now fill their
places, inherit much of their spirit of kindness
and hospitality.

W. SMITH ELLIOT, PRINTER, HIGH STREET, GALASHIELS.